A Ron Ransom Christmas

Patterns and Carving Tips for Santas, Snowmen, and More

Ron Ransom

Text written with and photography by Dawn Stoltzfus

Schiffer Publishing Ltd

4880 Lower Valley Road, Atglen, PA 19310 USA

To the Quarterly Tax Carving Club—you know who you are.

And to Penny and Alton Caudell, who are great travelling companions—also, Alton can drive at night.

Library of Congress Catalog Card Number: 97-80065

Book Design by: Laurie A. Smucker

ISBN: 0-7643-0361-9
Printed in China

Published by Schiffer Publishing Ltd.
4880 Lower Valley Road
Atglen, PA 19310
Phone: (610) 593-1777; Fax: (610) 593-2002
E-mail: schifferbk@aol.com
Please write for a free catalog.
This book may be purchased from the publisher.
Please include $3.95 for shipping.
Try your bookstore first.

We are interested in hearing from authors with book ideas on related subjects.

Contents

Foreword

by Nancy Goff

When I thank God for all of His many blessings, I try to remember to include Ron Ransom. His first book, *Santa Carving*, proved to be a major blessing in my life. Dramatic as that sounds, it's true. That book changed me from a housewife-with-a-hobby, who thought knives were for potatoes and basswood must have something to do with musical instruments, into a woman with a full-time career.

I had been using my time earning a little spare money painting and cutting out nice little flat shapes on my little scroll saw. When I saw *Santa Carving* with its charming Santas, wonderful photos, and clear instructions I knew in a flash that I could carve. I could carve! Off I went into a whole new world of learning, growing, and years of hard but satisfying work. Without that book, I would never have dreamed of using a big band saw, all those sharp tools, and caving things that people would want to buy.

As a rank beginner I loved Ron's books and wore them to shreds. Today each new one is an eagerly awaited delight. Talking to other carvers I know they value them as I do. Attending a carving show anywhere will show the enormous impact Ron has had on the carving world. He's a legend. And all of us followers have laughed out loud at his humor while finding out we can create joy as well as a Santa.

Now Ron has put together this new book, which will supply beginners with a solid start and more advanced carvers with the encouragement to keep going, try something new, and improve our skills. However we use this book I know it will be a good experience. Isn't that what it's all about—enjoying every minute of working, learning, and creating?

Thank you Ron. May all your Band-Aids be unused.

Introduction

I have received quite a few letters and photos from my carving friends from all around the country. A few of the letters gave me credit or blame for getting involved with carving.

One of my favorite letters was from Nancy Goff of Missouri, who in eleven pages told me of her trials and tribulations on finding a decent knife and learning to sharpen it. She sent me wonderful photos of her carvings—Santas surrounded by animals and birds, Noah's Arks and whimsical angels that I wished I had thought of first. Nancy is represented by a top-notch gallery in the Chicago, Illinois, area and was recently featured in *Home* magazine. I appreciate Nancy doing the forward for this book.

I hope you can find one or two Santa patterns that you can use. After the Mini-cheers book came out I had requests for snowmen (or women, if one can tell the sex of a snowperson) patterns. My wife encouraged me to do snowpeople several years ago. They have been good sellers for me.

Enjoy, and, as usual, let me hear from you.

Ron Ransom
Box 4101
Marietta, GA 30061

Please enclose a self-addressed, stamped envelope if you want an answer.

Tools

Those of you who have used my other books know that I mostly use a knife. Don't be concerned with all the tools shown here. Sometimes they help move some wood, but a knife alone will be fine.

Each pattern shown in this book will be pretty much from start to finish, so, if you want to skip from pattern to pattern, go ahead. I've moved the tools out of my way and now we will begin to carve the slender Santa.

The tools we will be using.

Flexcut gouges.

The "Slender Santa"

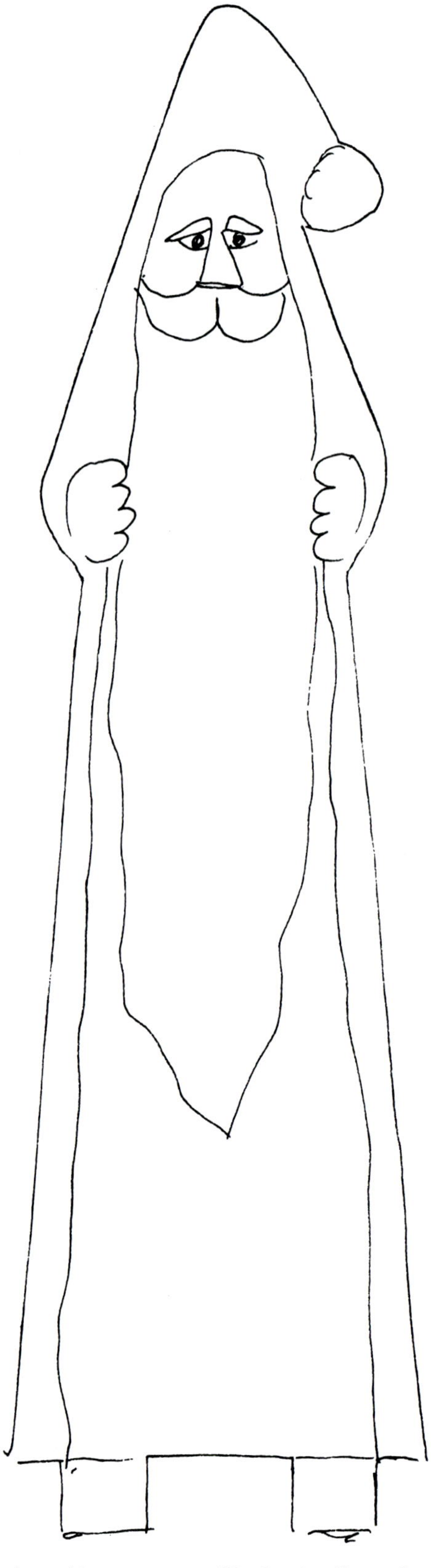

Two versions of this Santa you could carve, shown with pattern traced and cut out on wood.

The first pattern we will do is the slender Santa. He evolved from having slender scraps left over from some larger pieces done earlier.

Starting on the back of the Santa we carve under the arm.

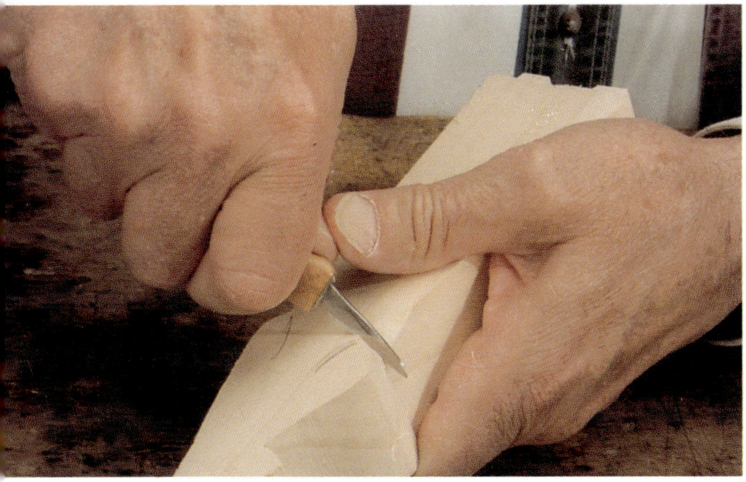

Notice my thumb pushing on the other thumb for leverage.

The robe is beginning to be rounded.

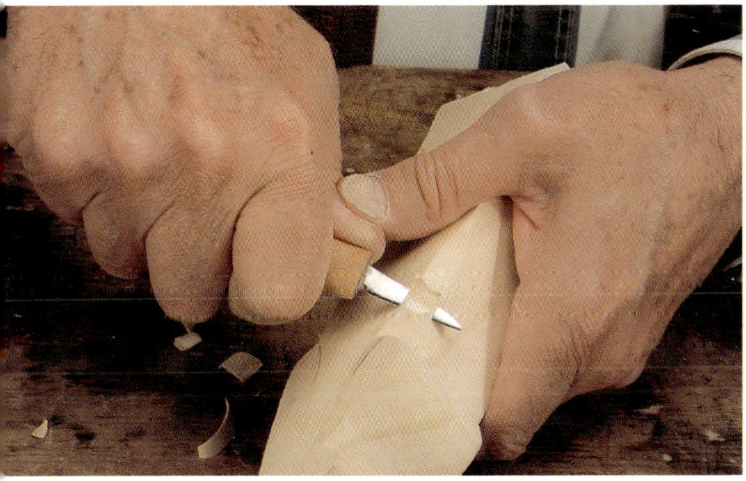

Begin to take out small pieces.

After you've rounded a bit you may want to make a reference and round up to that line so that you don't go too far.

Begin rounding the robe up to the arm.

The grain of basswood is very subtle, so you may turn your piece over from time to time to carve with the grain.

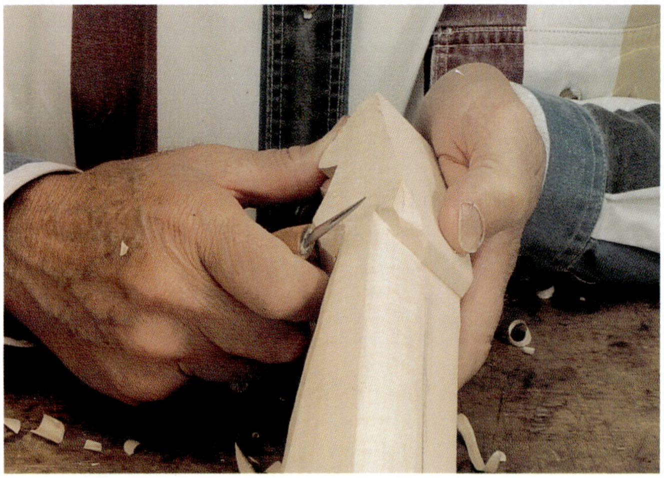

Round off the back of the both arms.

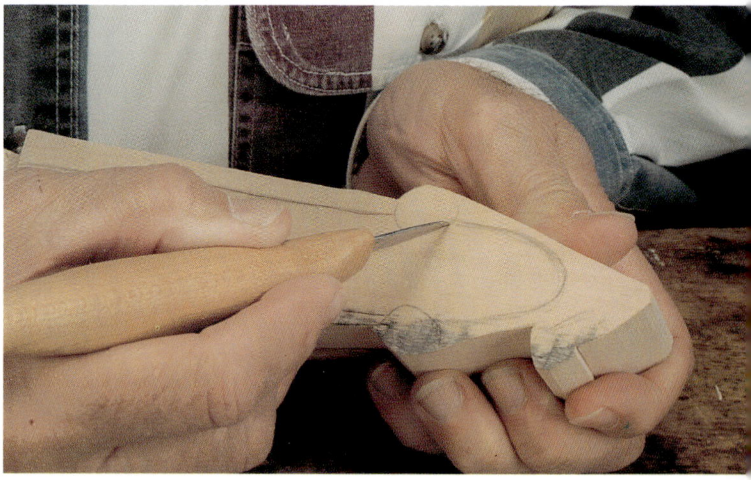

Also incise around the hands.

Continue rounding each side of the back of Santa.

Incise each side of the robe.

Incise the lines on the beard, going as deep as you can.

Gently round each of the front lines up to the beard, following your incise lines.

Notice that there are still saw marks on the sides but we can take them off later.

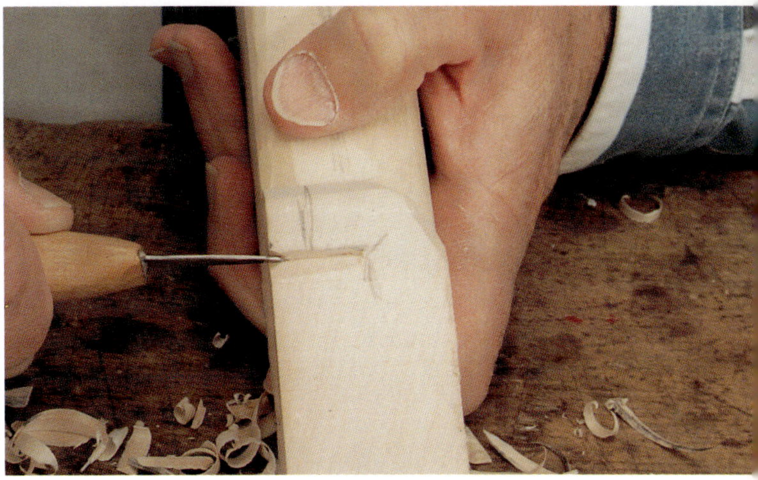

Make a v cut, which is done by an incision in the shape of a v.

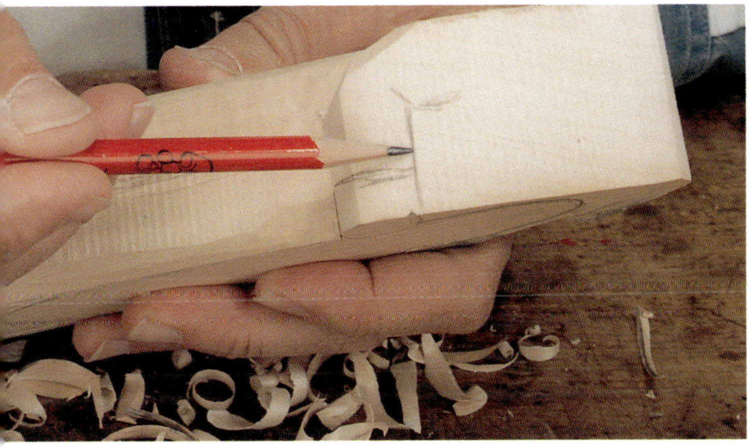

Draw in lines for the hands and arms on the sides.

Round the back of the arms on both sides.

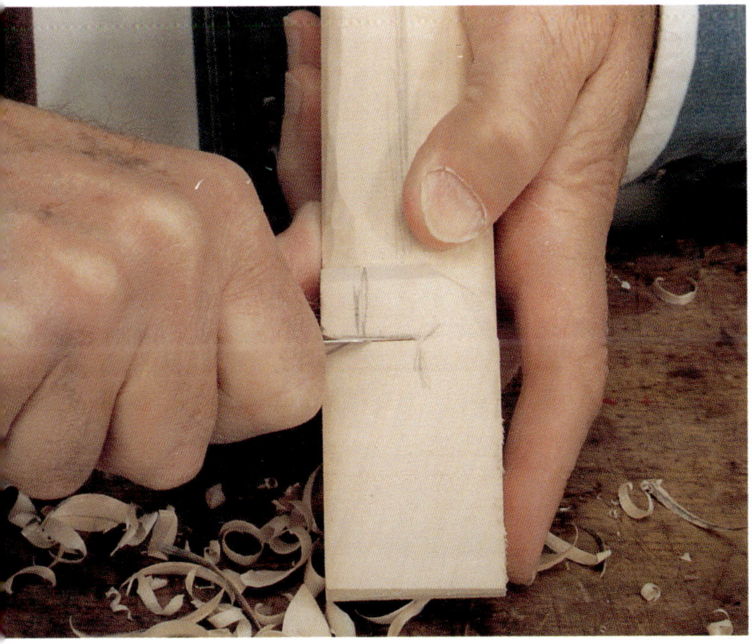

Also incise the arm.

Draw in the ball cap of the robe on Santa.

Color in the area of wood which you will be taking off.

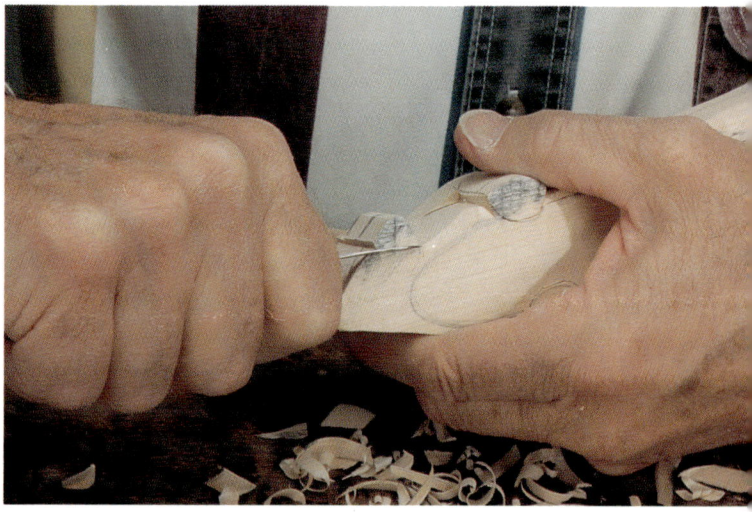

To carve the ball out you make a little cut and then start to take off the wood.

At this point, I need to stop and sharpen my knife. I am holding a strip of smooth leather glued onto a piece of wood which I use to do this.

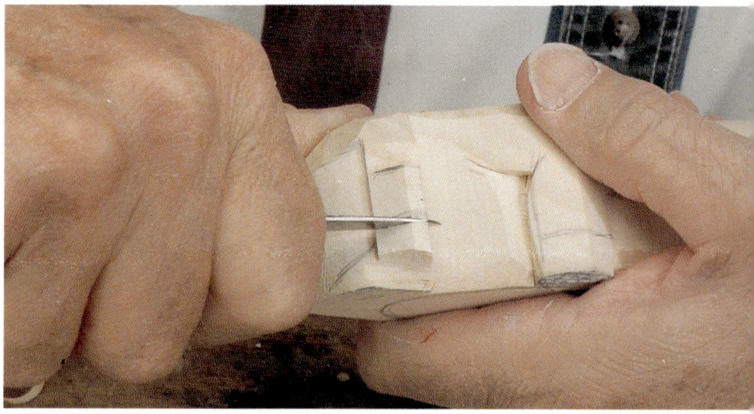

Continue to take off the wood.

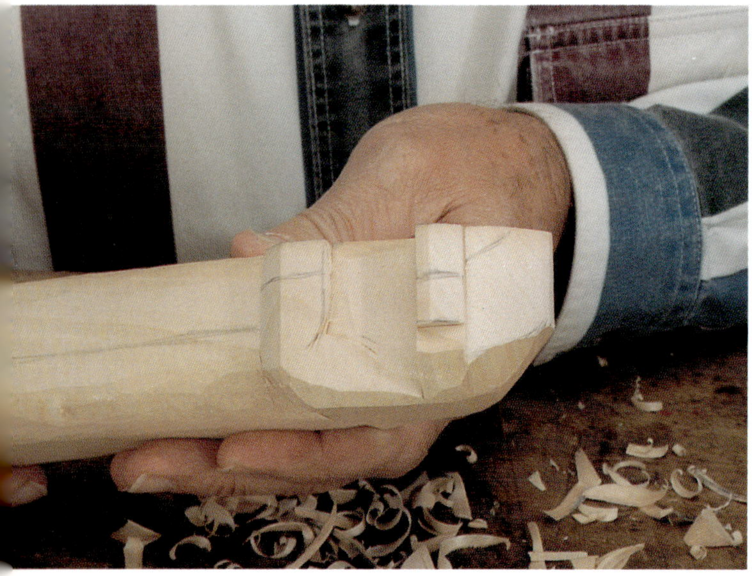

Round the top of the robe and carve out around the ball of the cap.

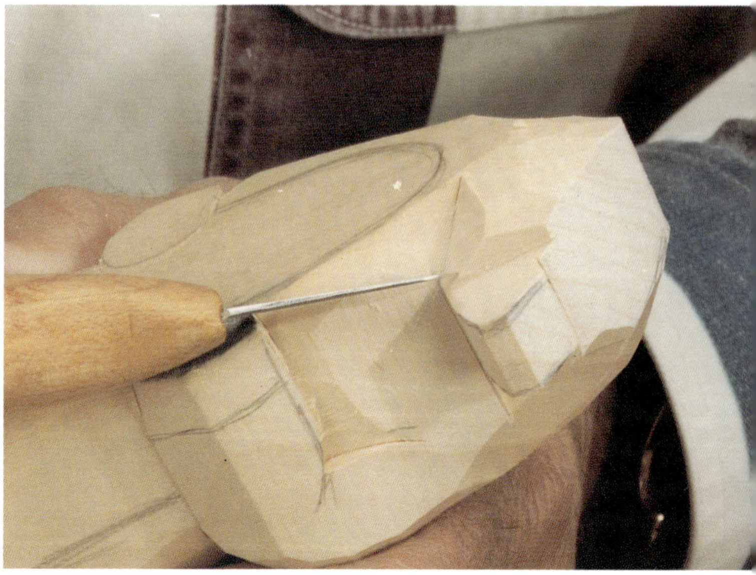

Cut away to the size ball you want and now round it.

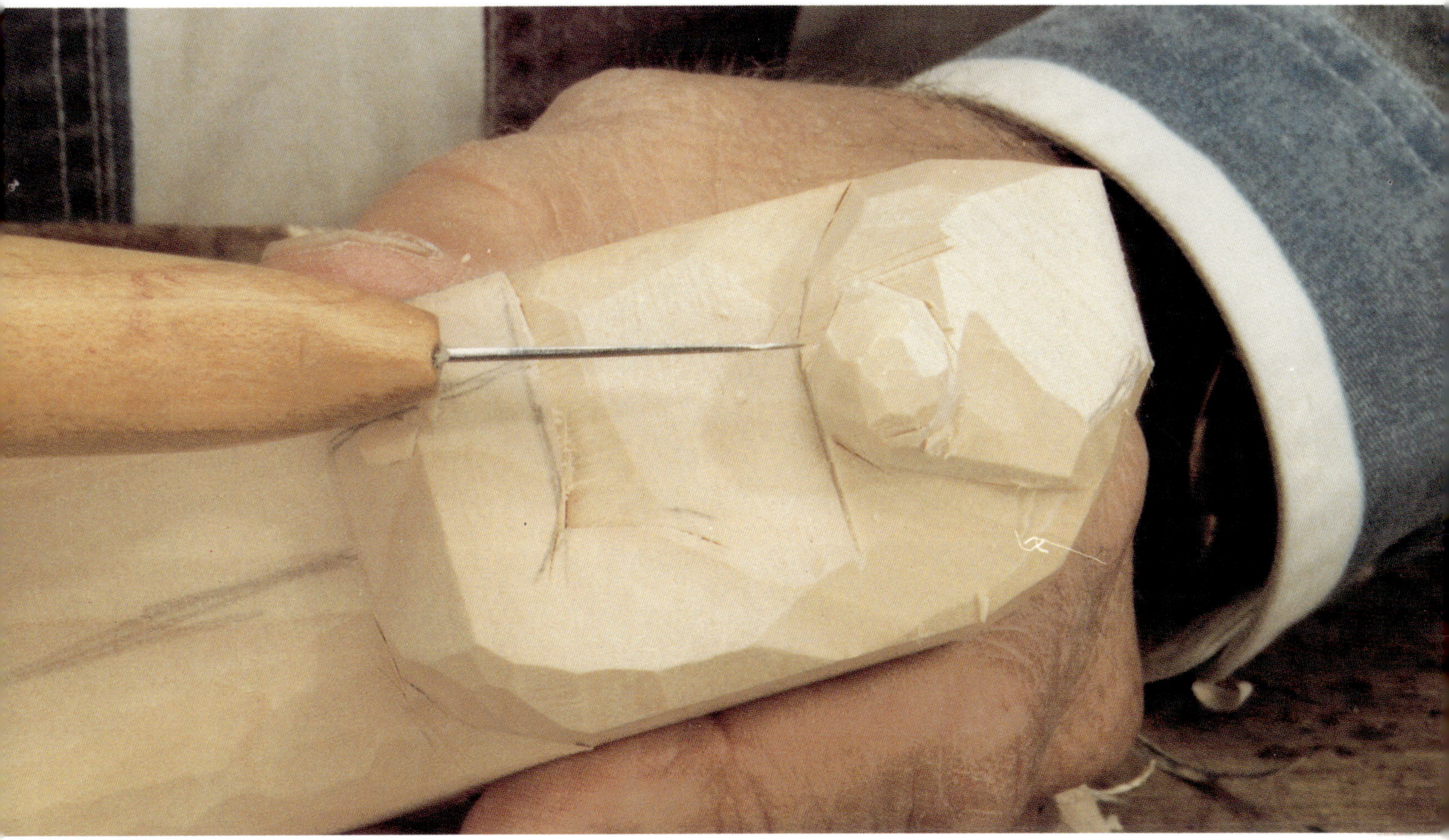

We have rounded the ball.

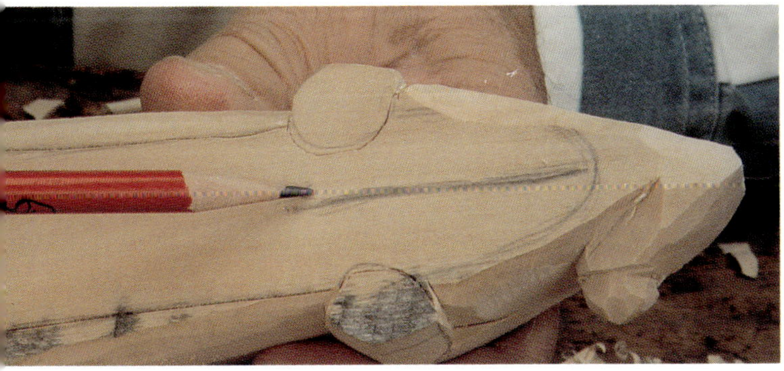

Draw another line down the center.

Round up to the facial area.

Round up to the center line.

Incise the end of each hand.

Cut around where the hand goes into the robe.

Continue working on the hands.

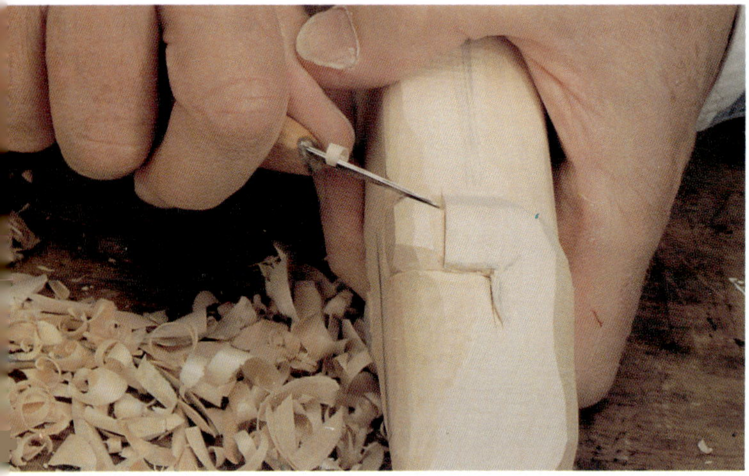

Do both hands the same.

Decide at this point if you want fingers or mittens, if you want fingers then the small v-gouge is very handy.

Take off the sharp edges on the hands.

Here you can see I have used the v-gouge to carve a groove for fingers on the hand.

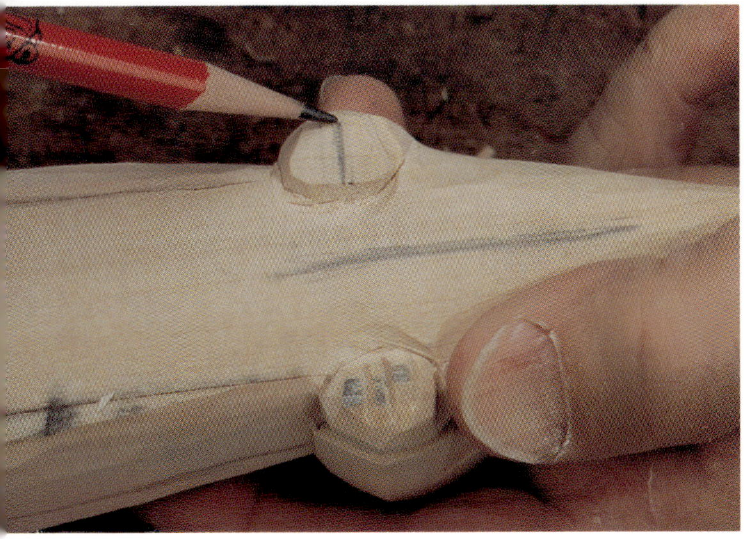

If you are doing the fingers with a knife then draw a pencil line in the middle of the hand and then draw in the fingers on each side.

Use the gouge to define the beard.

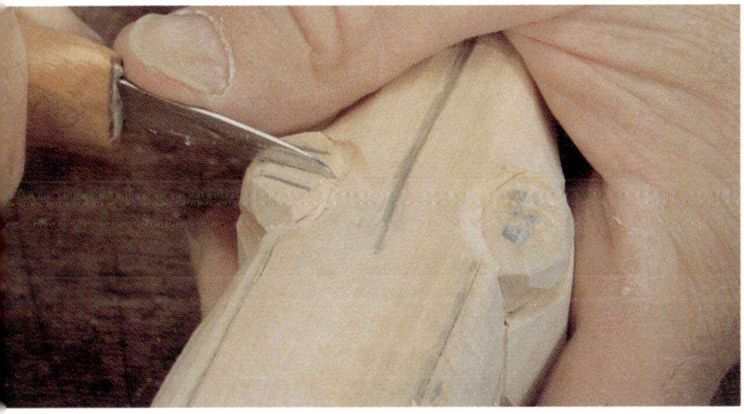

Put your knife on the middle line that you've drawn and rock it back and forth.

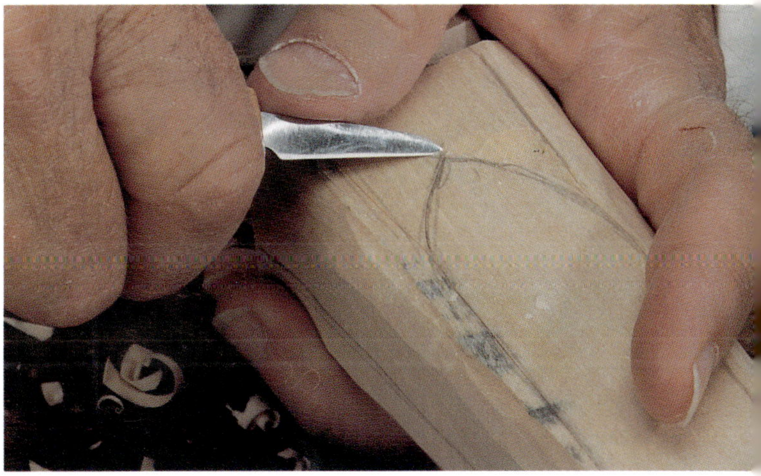

Here is how to use the knife to define the beard if you do not have a gouge.

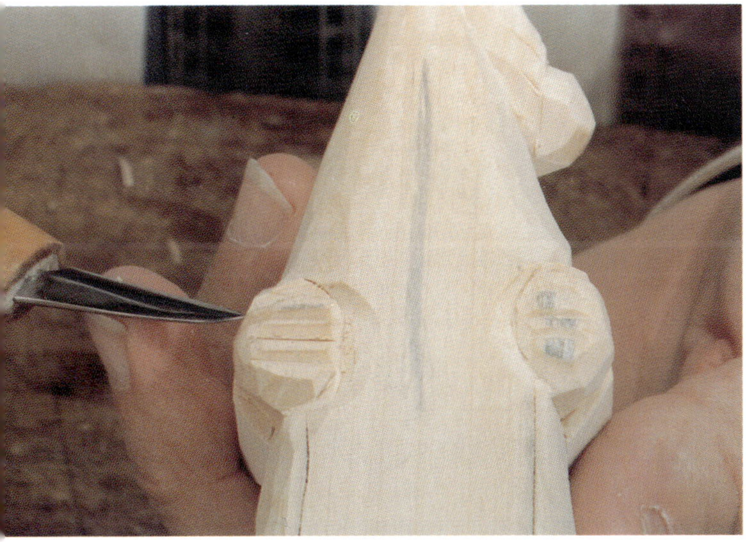

This is how it will look done with the knife. The knife hand is on the left and the gouge hand is on the right.

Lay the blade flat to the surface, push with your thumb next to the line that you previously incised.

I have rounded the gown into the robe.

Take out around the beard and under the fingers on each side.

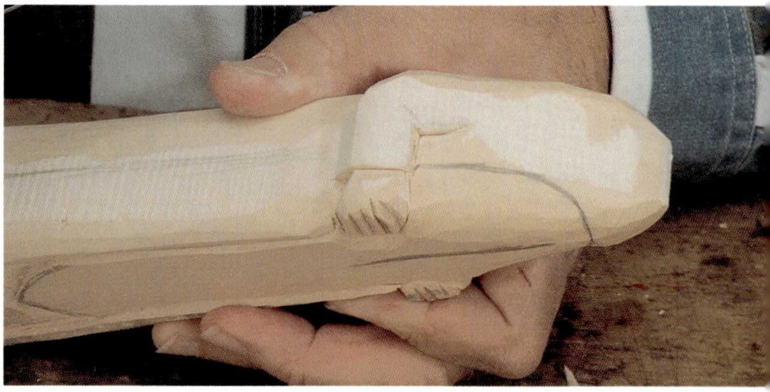

This is an important step: draw the line for the face.

I have cut around the beard.

Draw the line all the way around.

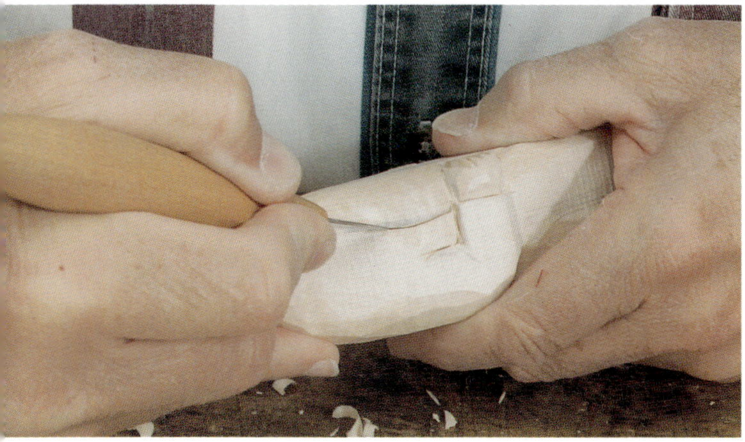

Incise all the way around the line, fairly deep.

Doing the face: first draw a horizontal line across the eye area.

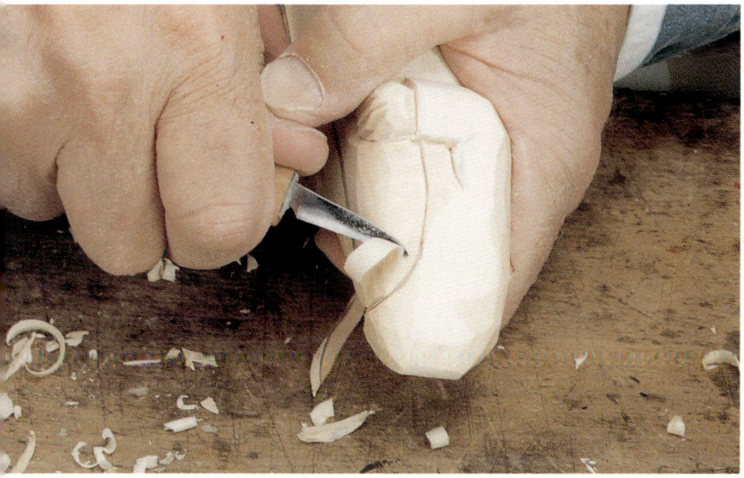

Now you're beginning to get the egg shape that you need to do the face.

The next step is a nice triangular shaped nose, make it plenty wide.

Continue to round up to the center line.

Now draw a nice round cheek line which goes all the way up.

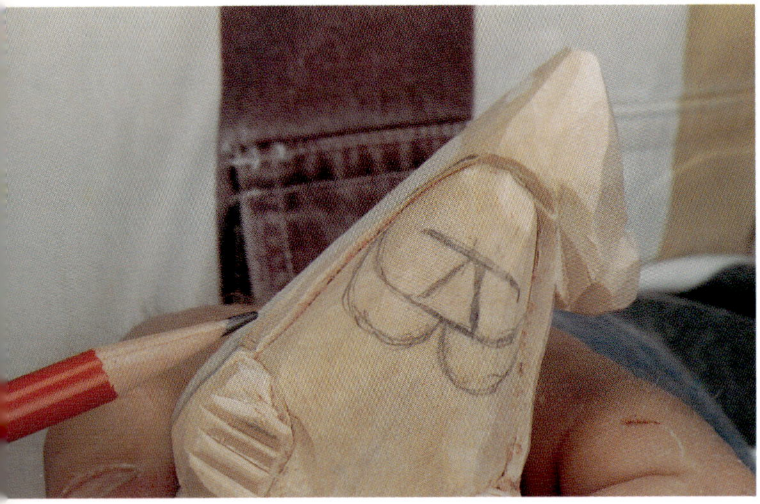

Draw the mustache.

The eyebrows.

Take your knife and rock it back and forth on the line under the eyebrows.

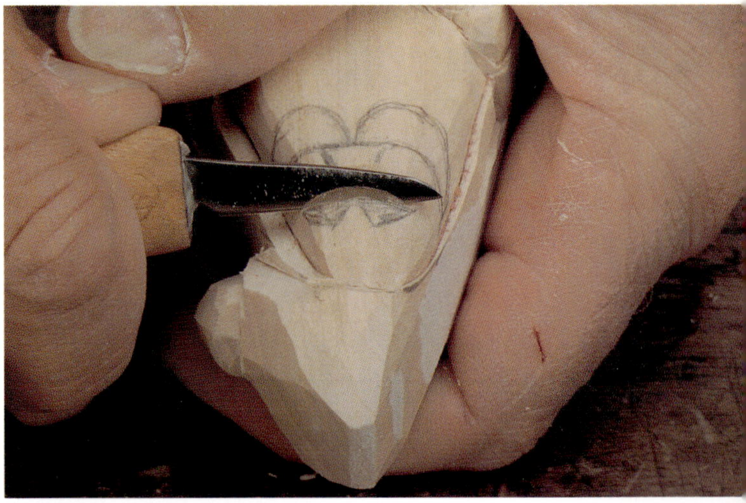

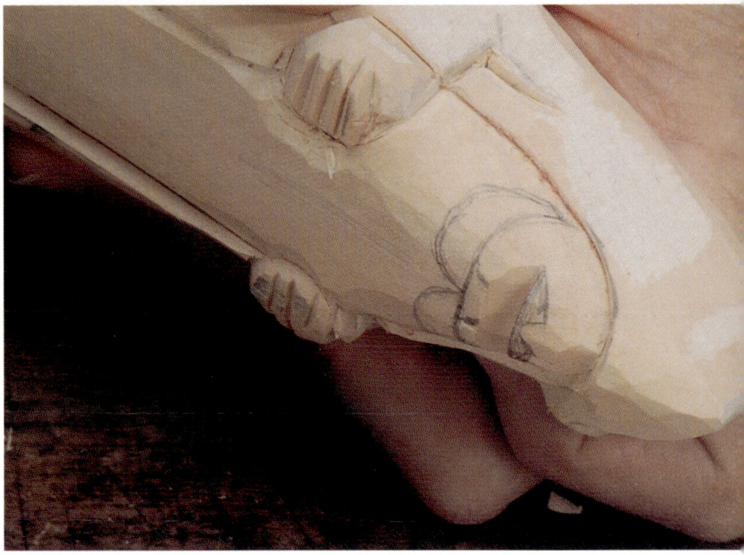

Cut on an angle up to the original horizontal cut. Make another and carefully trim out.

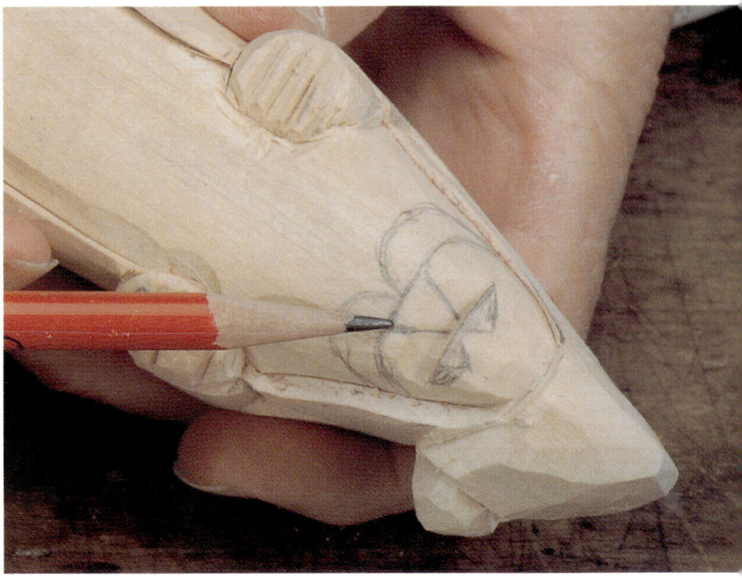

While you're there, draw nose lines back in.

Deeply cut each nose line.

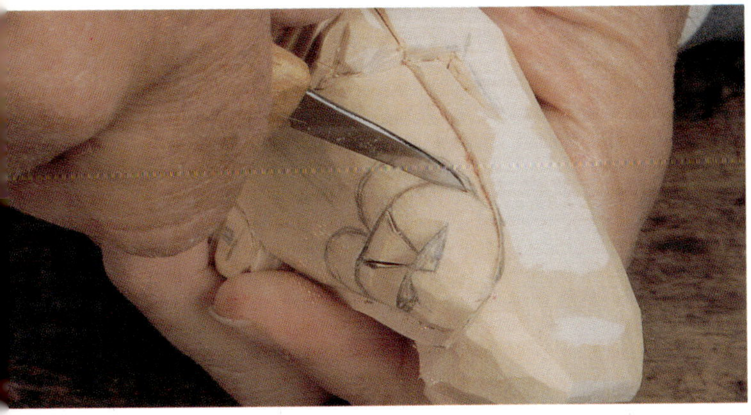

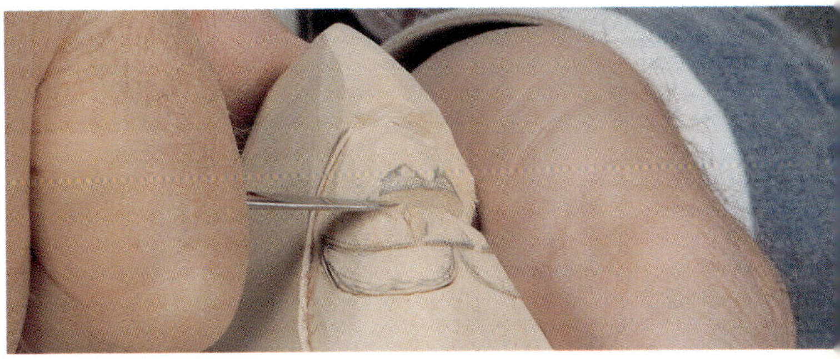

Cut out around the nose, each side.

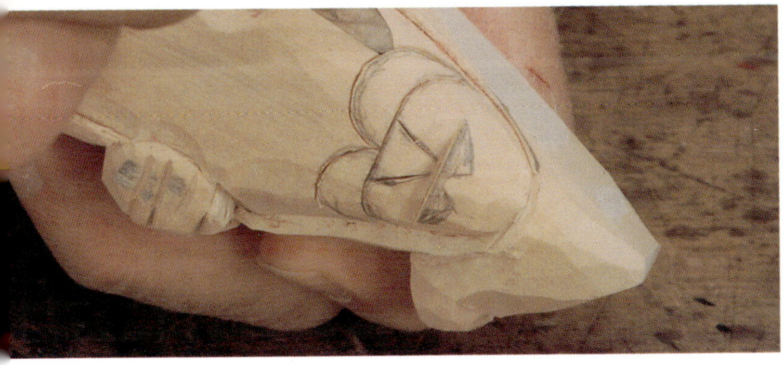

Incise around the moustache.

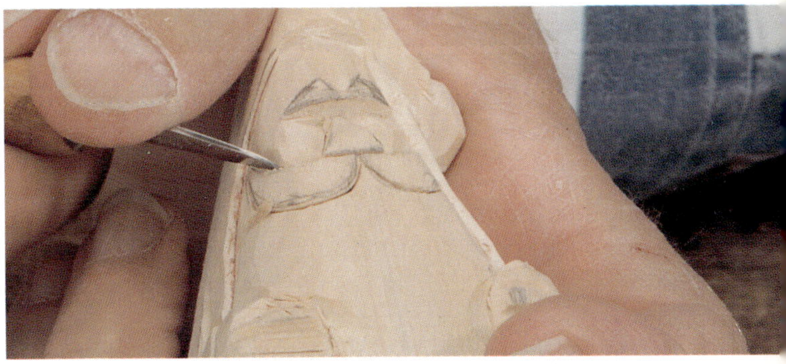

Round each side of the cheek.

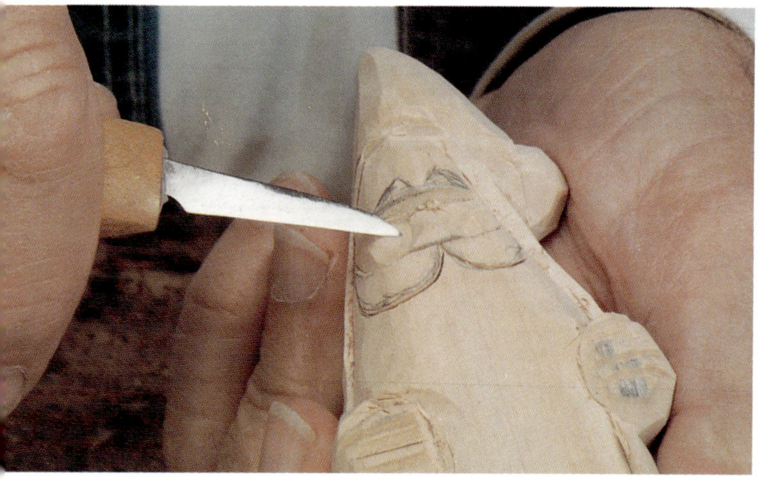

Round each side of the nose.

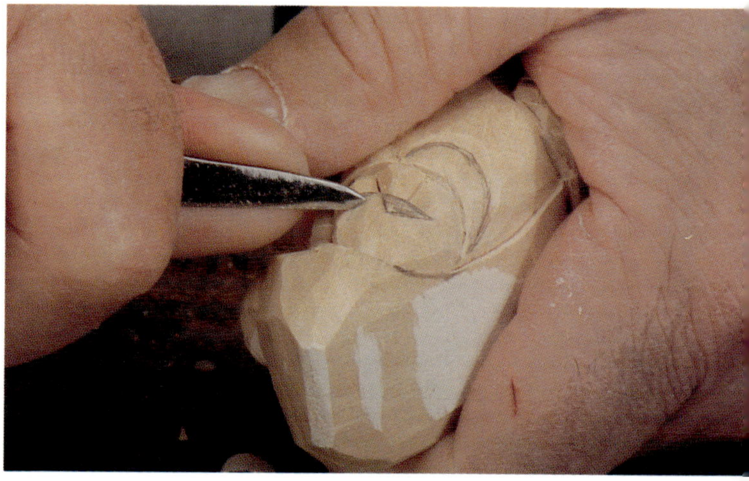

This is a very delicate move: incise around the area you have drawn in for the eyebrows.

This is important, people often forget to take a little nip off of each side of the nose to help give it some "nose look".

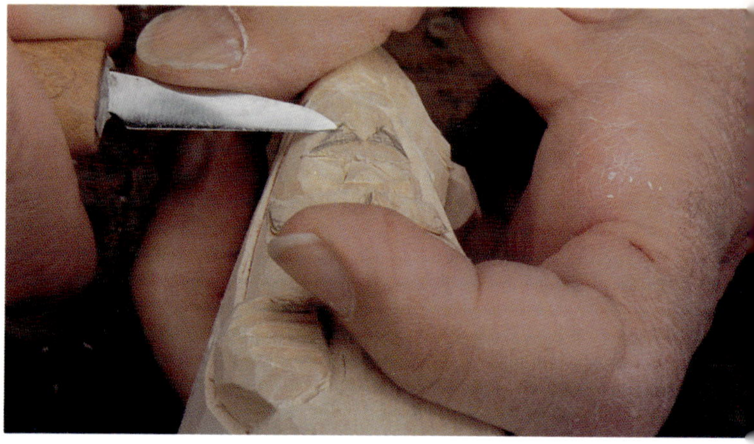

Very carefully take out a small area around the eyebrow up to where you have incised. Be very careful because the eyebrow could chip off easily here.

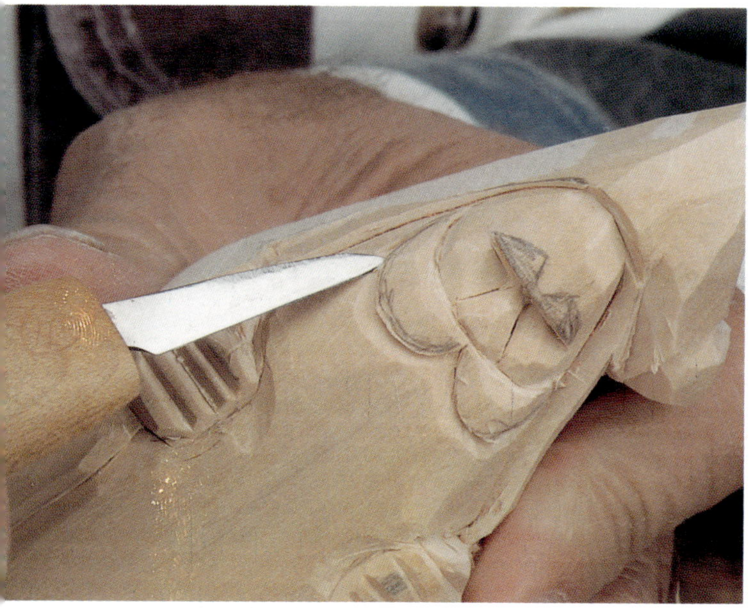

Trim under the mustache.

I have drawn in the eyes.

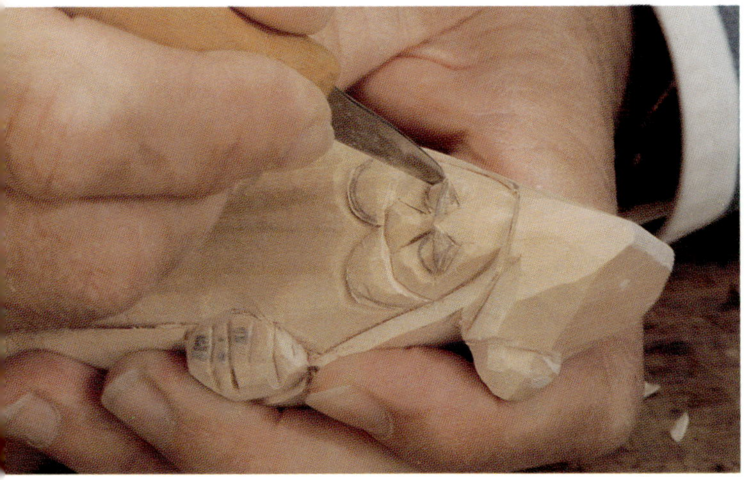

Put the blade in the corner of the eye very deeply.

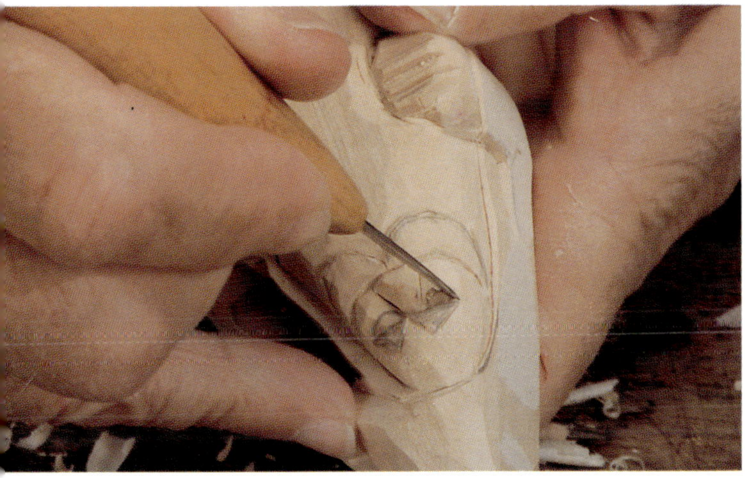

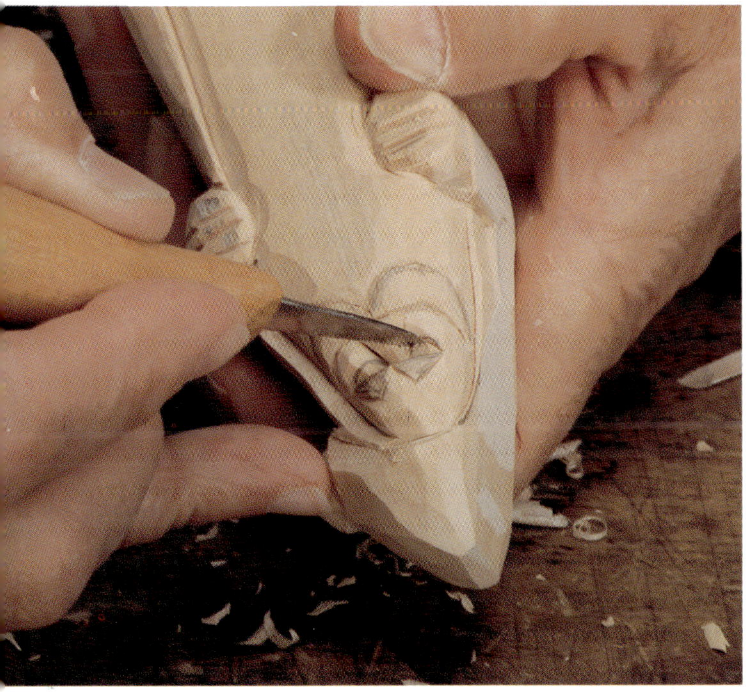

With the thumb, follow the pencil line to the other side of the eye and then stick the point of the blade in deeply there.

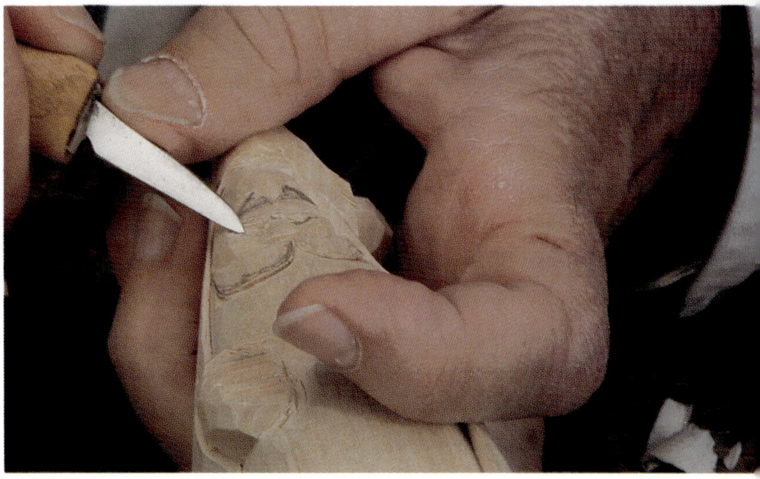

Very carefully take out a small piece on the side of each eye.

Now for the beard: draw squiggly lines for the beard.

If you are using a knife, incise one of the lines you have drawn.

Then come back and take out the piece which you have just incised.

With a small v-gouge you can also make a similar line, so you may use whichever method you choose.

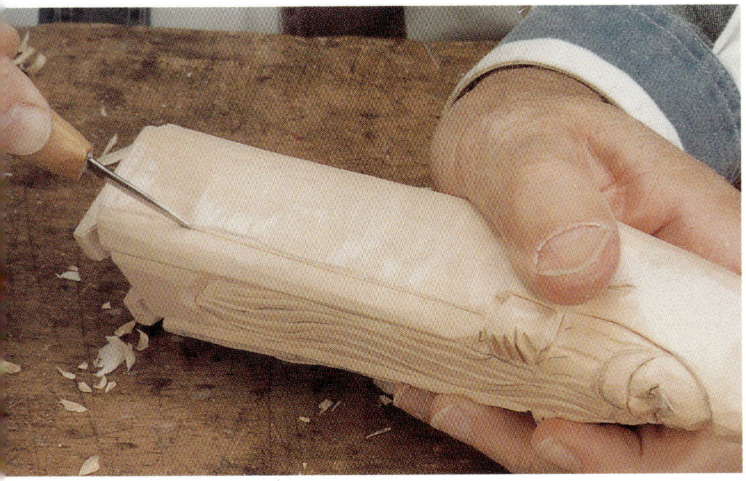

To put some fur trim on the robe just incise a line from one end to the other.

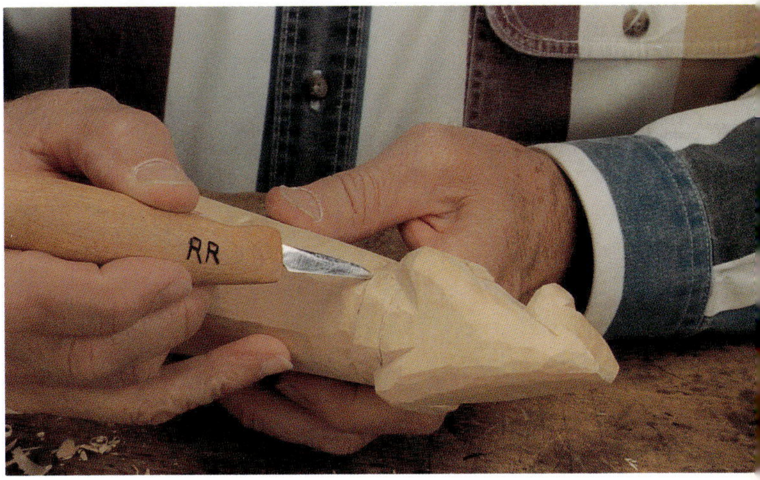

I decided this robe was too long, and so I added a belt. Use the same technique as you used to do the fur. Take time now to round the feet up and touch up other areas.

Lay the blade flat and take out the piece to define the fur, then repeat the fur on the other side.

To give the face a little more character, carve a v into each eye to give Santa some laughter lines.

Add fur on each sleeve.

Add little wrinkle lines in the robe on the back. Make an incision in the line and trim away from each side.

Santa with Torch

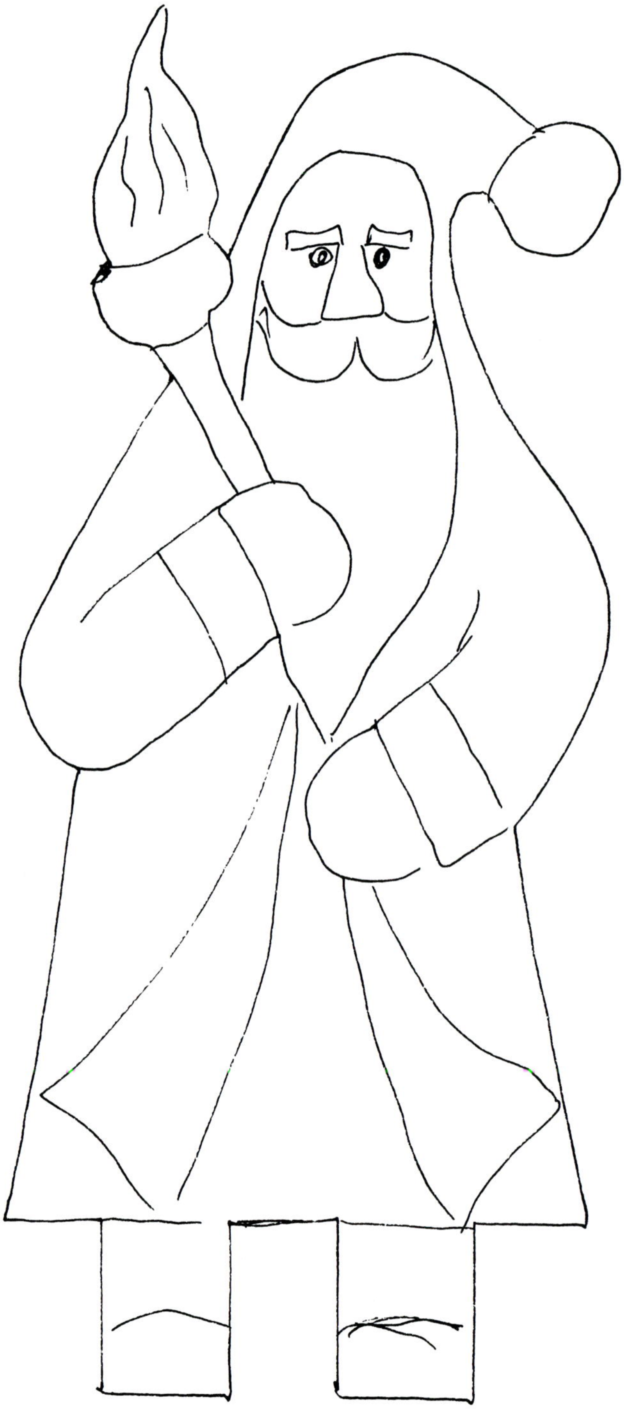

Finished Santa with cut out.

Use the big fishtail gouge behind the torch because it can take large pieces of wood.A Foredom can also be used to do this.

Starting with the back, make a nice healthy v cut under the arms.

Make healthy v-cuts on each side.

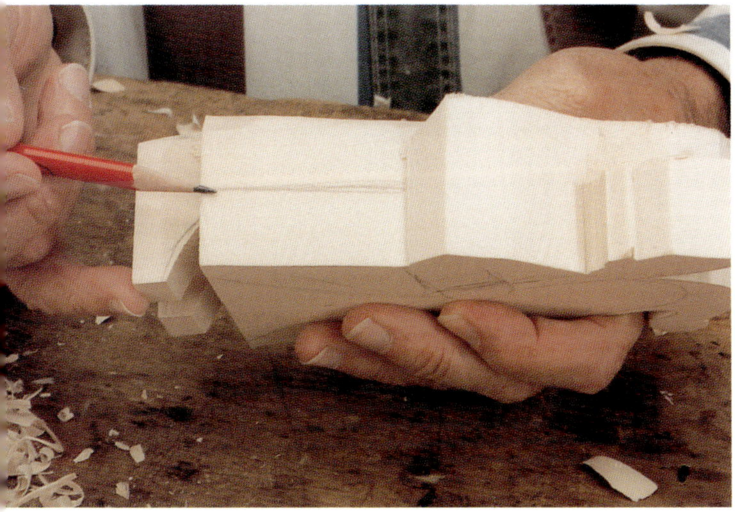

Draw a line down the center of the robe.

Round towards the center line.

Make cuts under the front elbow.

Round the front of the robe towards the middle line you have drawn. After teaching hundreds of students and wondering why their pieces kept ending up so skinny, I realized they were taking the side off and kept rounding down. You need to draw a line in the center, and leave it there. Do not cut down that line. You need to just round to it.

To get the definition on the back of the arms, make a nice pencil line, and a nice deep incision.

Trim out the wood in the shape of a v.

Begin to round off the back of the arms.

Begin to round off the back of the robe.

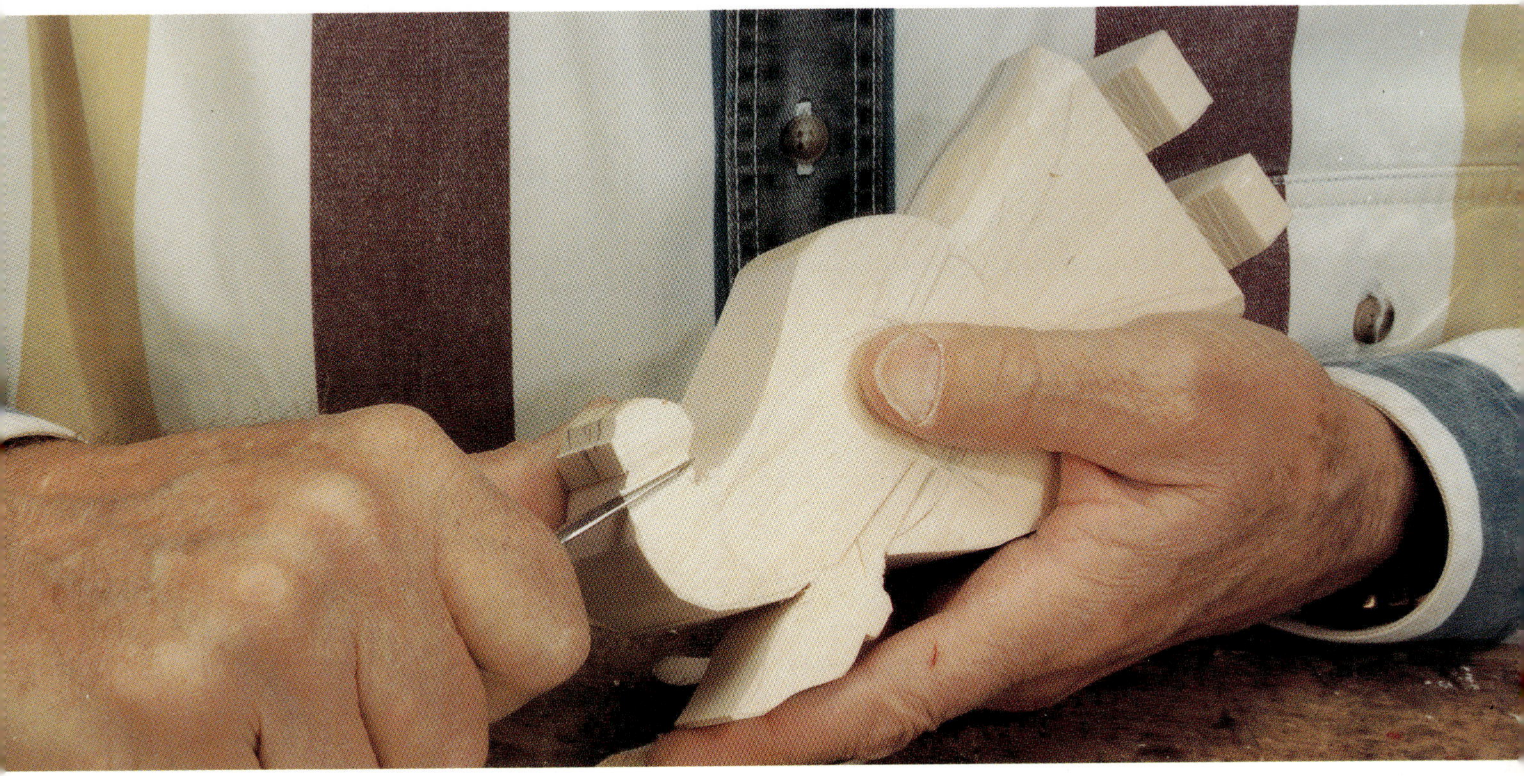

Make a series of v-cuts to get the shape of the ball of the cap.

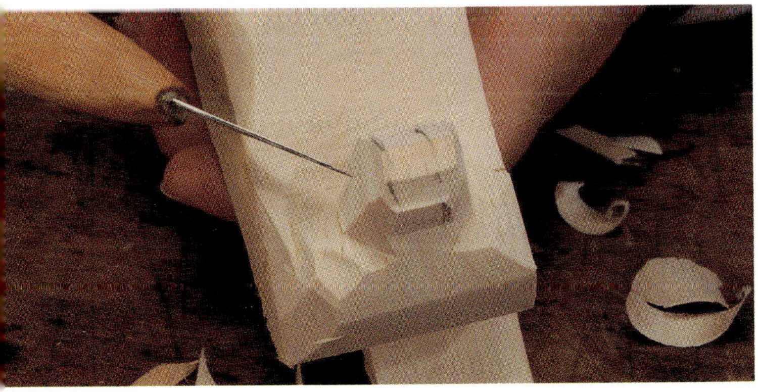

Keep rounding the ball.

Incise the lines for both hands and the torch.

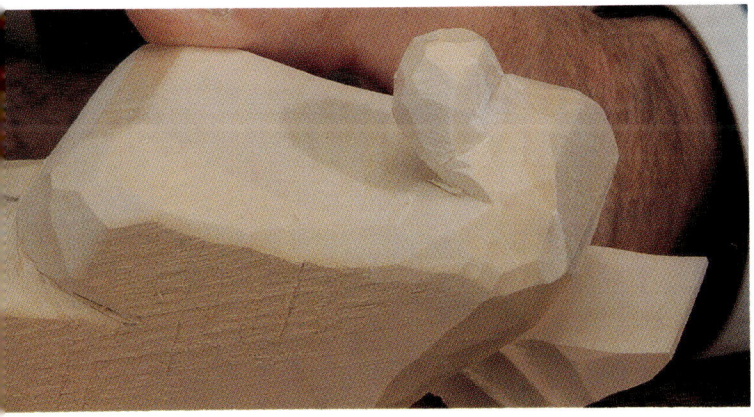

I have finished the ball and am now beginning to work on the back of the head.

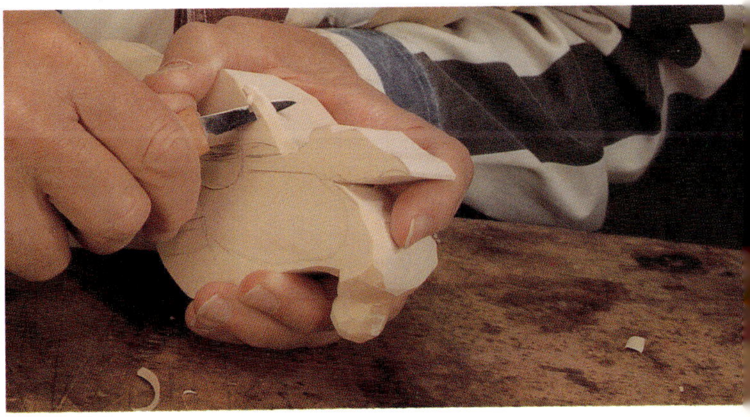

Start carving away towards the torch.

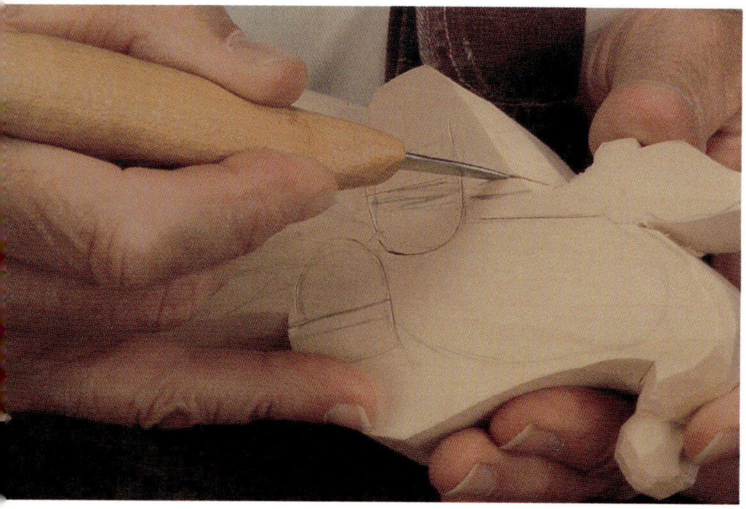

Incise where the beard comes under the torch on the right side.

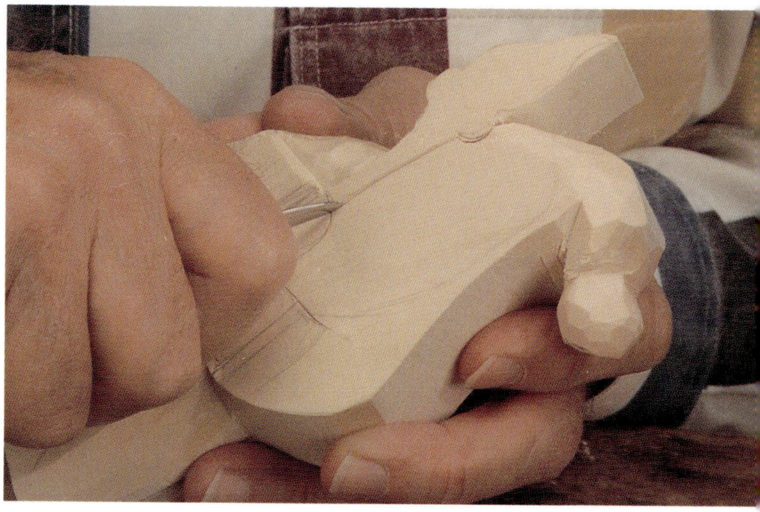

Relieve the torch from the side of the face.

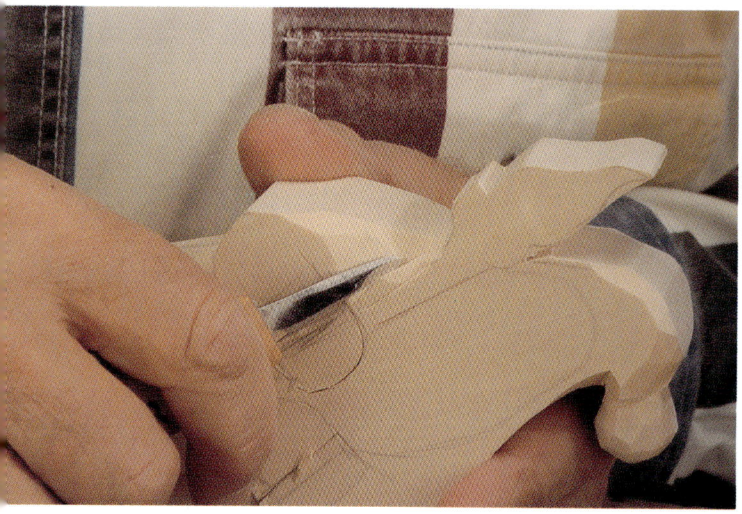

Trim around where the aforementioned beard meets the torch.

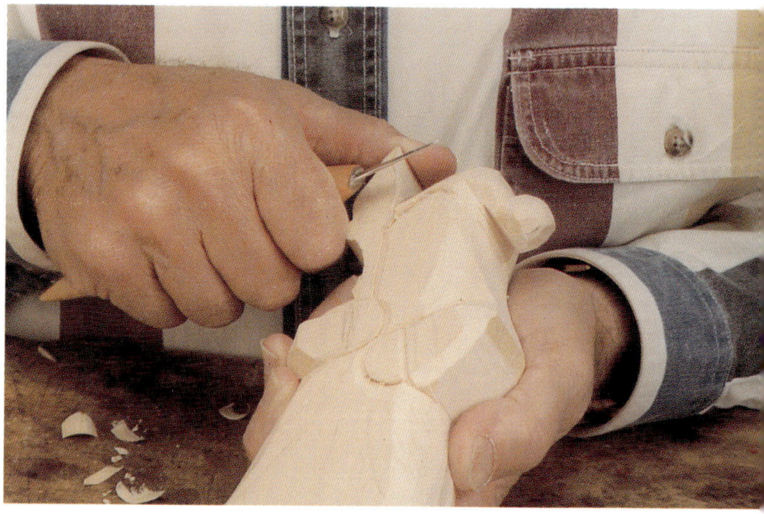

Begin to take away some of the face and define the arms as it comes up by the face.

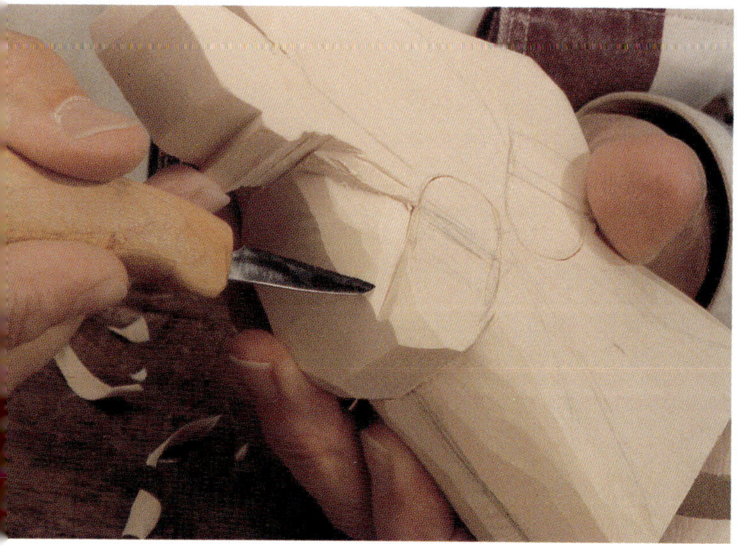

Begin to shape the arm.

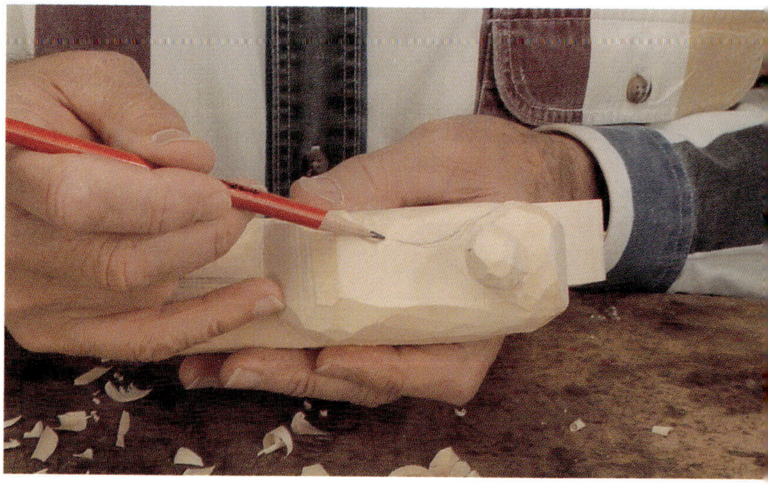

Now is a good time to put the other line of the face in, so you won't take away too much of it as you take away from the arm.

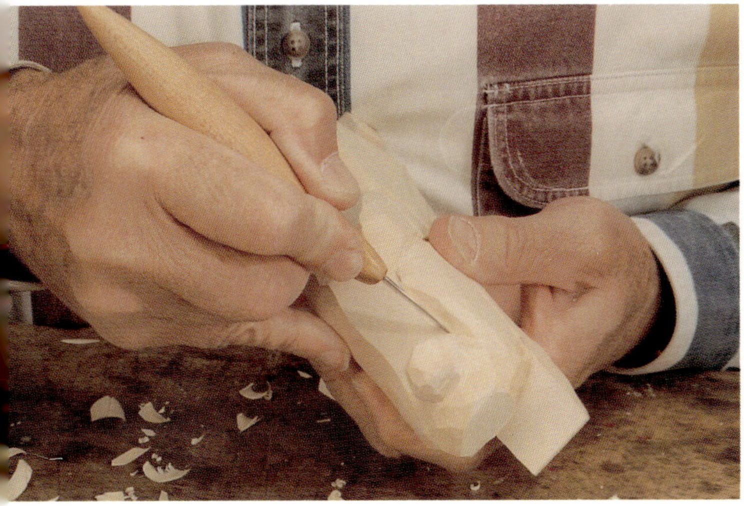

Now, as in the previous Santa, cut away from the line.

Begin to work on the torch. Incise the line on the top of the torch where the flame comes from.

Start to round the face.

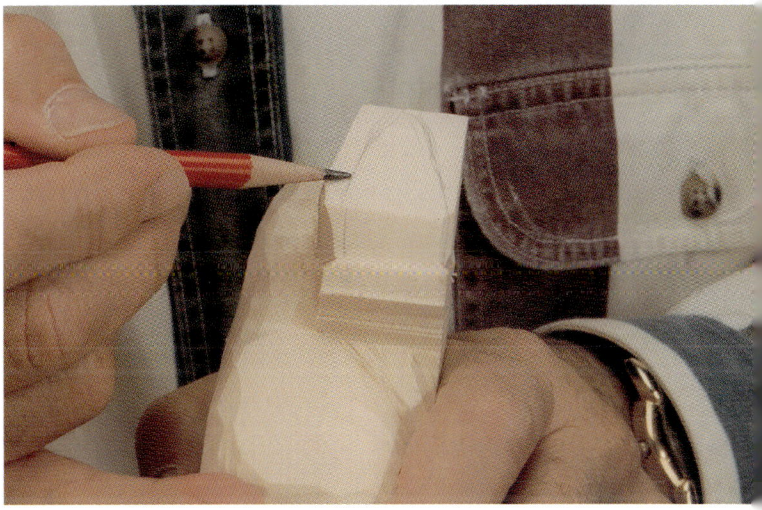

You may want to draw lines to show where the wood will need to come off from the torch.

Continue to round the arm.

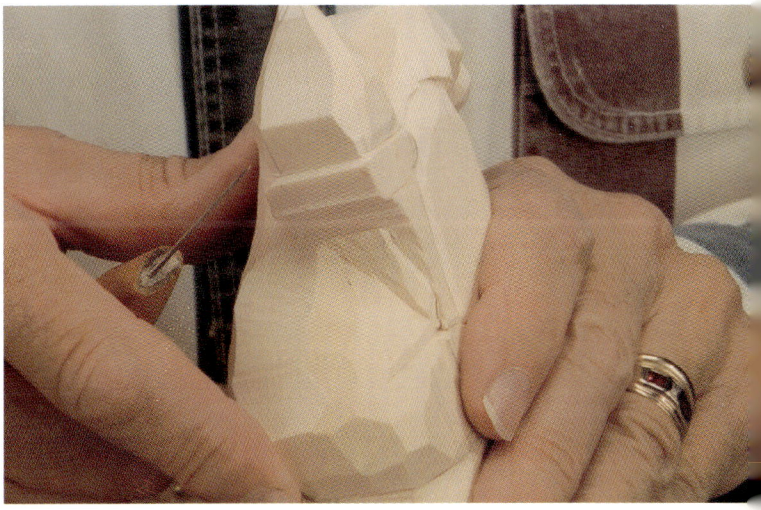

Round the torch—as I have never seen a square flame! Trim up the flame.

Continue to round all over the piece.

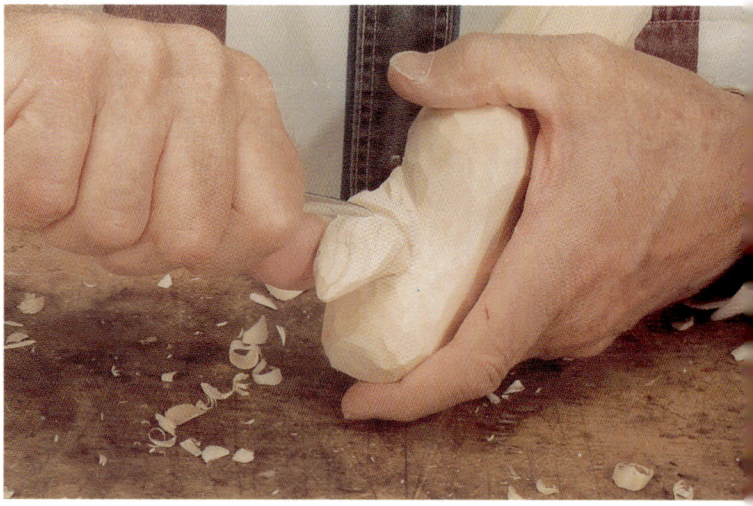

Incise the line that you just drew in.

Use a fishtail gouge on the back of the Santa to take off saw marks. This can also be done with sandpaper.

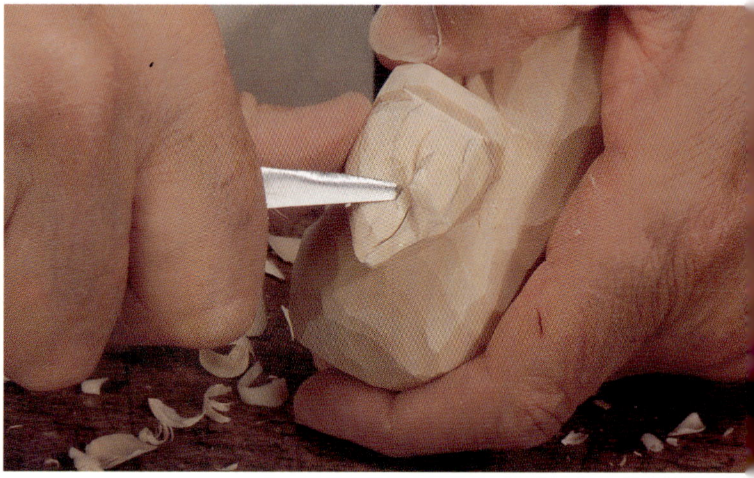

Lay the blade flat and take out the piece that you just incised.

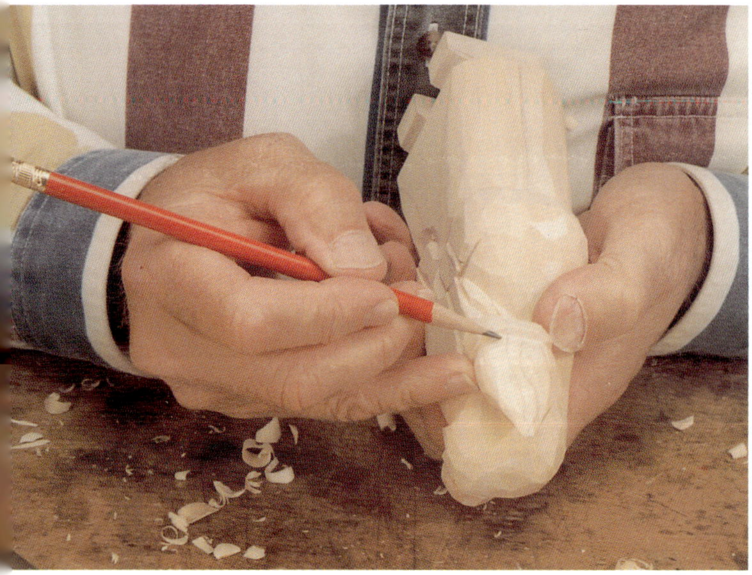

It may make things easier for you to draw in some flame lines on the torch.

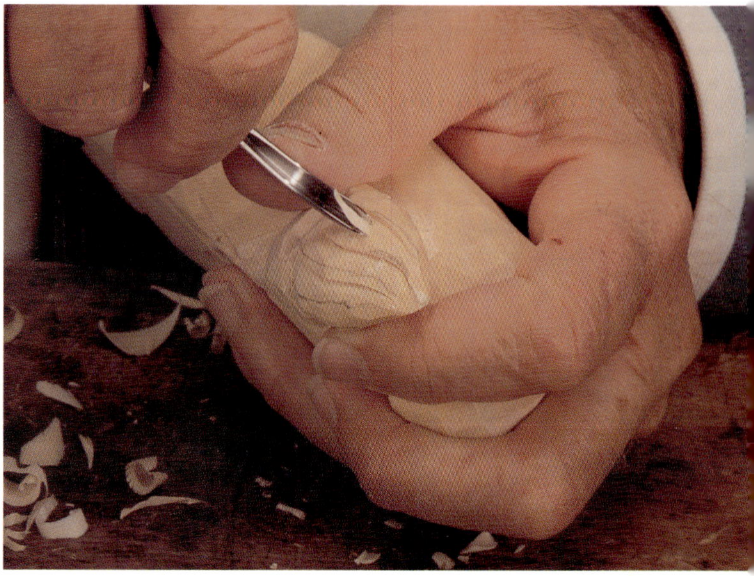

Or, if you have a gouge you may use it to make the flames, like so.

The flame is now detailed and ready to paint.

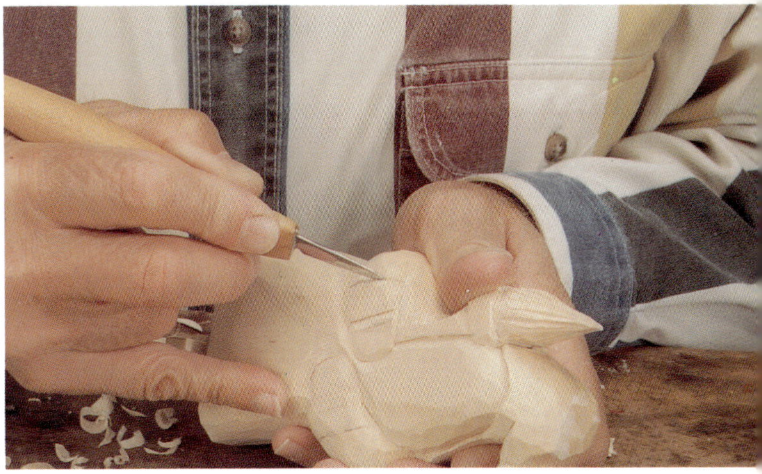

Put some fur on the sleeve by incising the line drawn there. Repeat on the other sleeve.

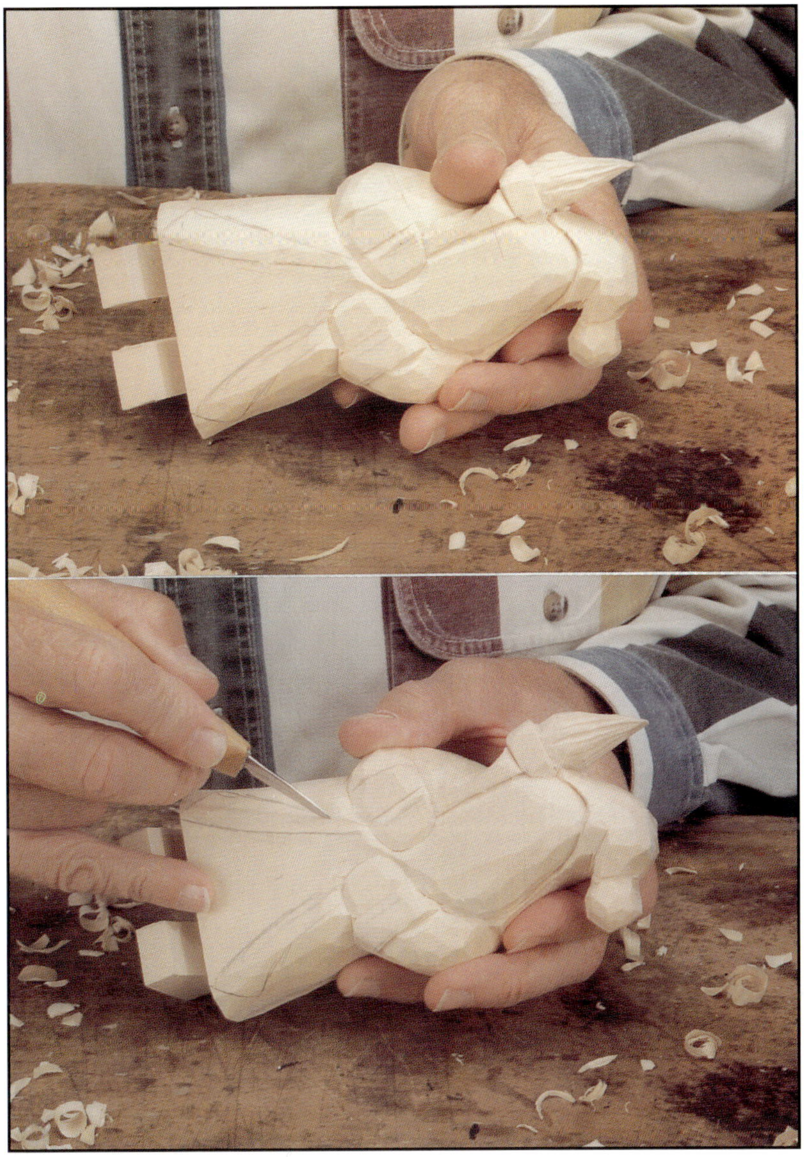

Draw the lines for the robe to flare and incise them.

Take out the area around the robe flap.

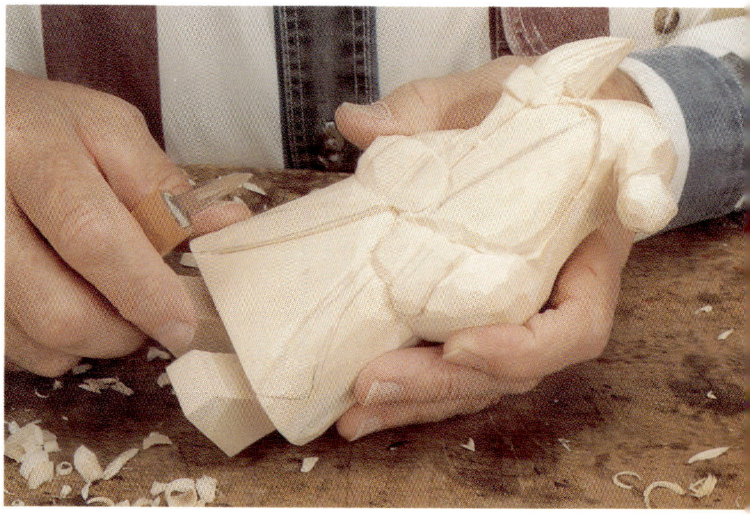

Continue to round the beard and face area.

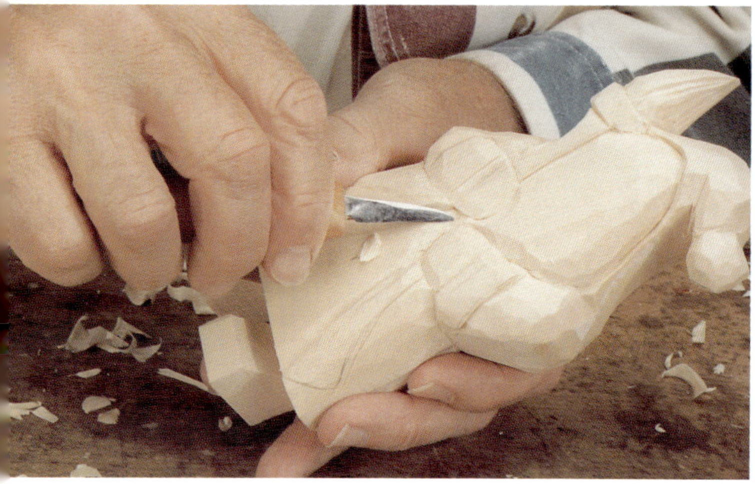

Cut a little piece between the hand and the beard to make it stand out.

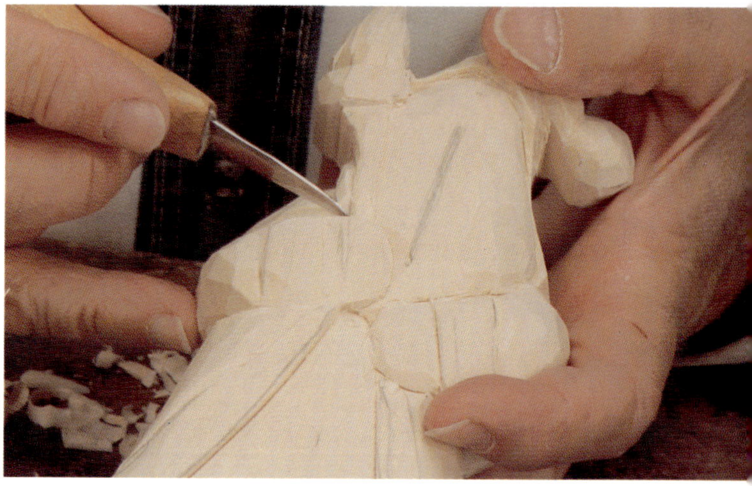

Round the torch and make sure it goes into the hand with a definite cut.

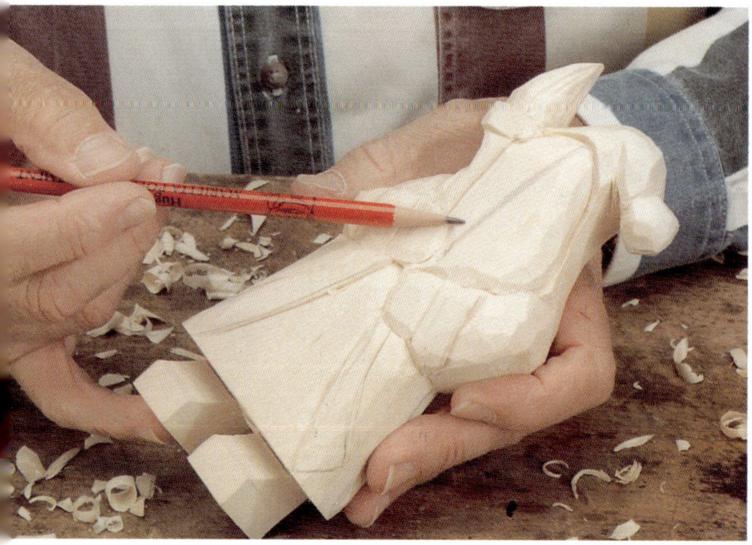

Draw a center line on the face so we'll know where to round it to.

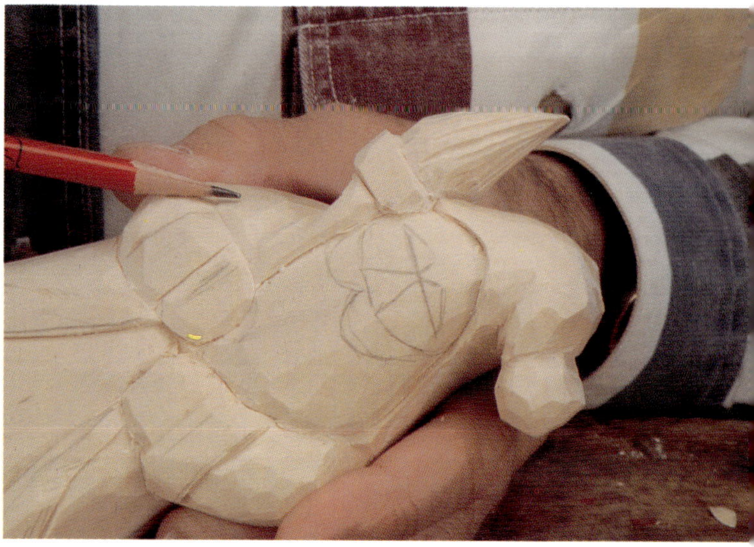

Once again, this is obviously a larger face but we will do this similar to the first Santa. Draw in a horizontal line, a wide nose, cheeks, eyes, and mustache.

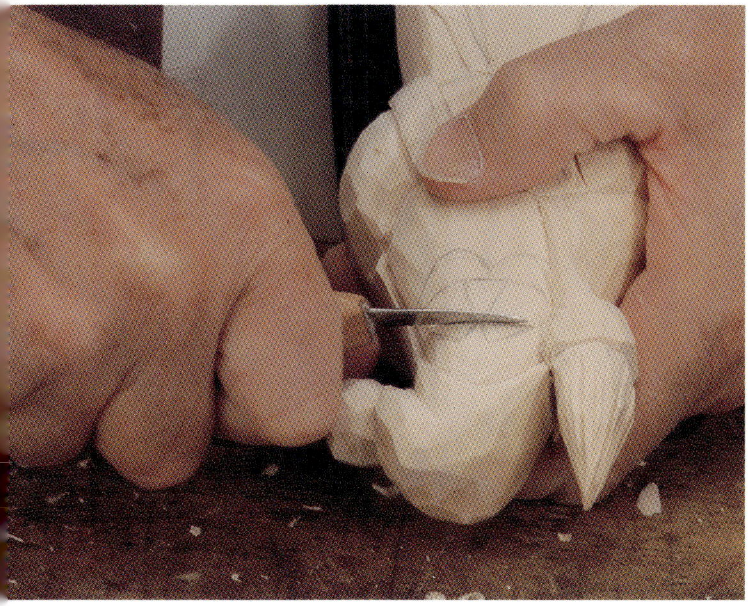

Remember the old trick of rocking your blade across the horizontal line.

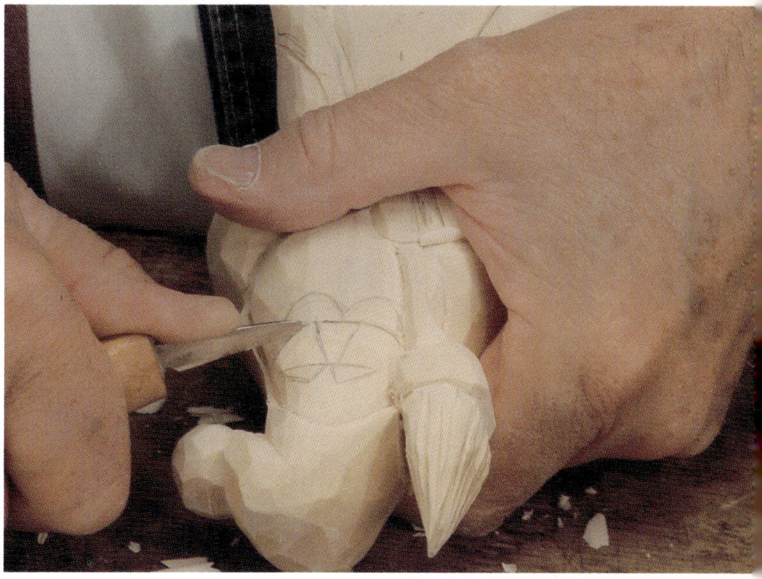

Do a nice round sweeping cut across the top of the mustache.

Round up to that line and draw your wide nose back in.

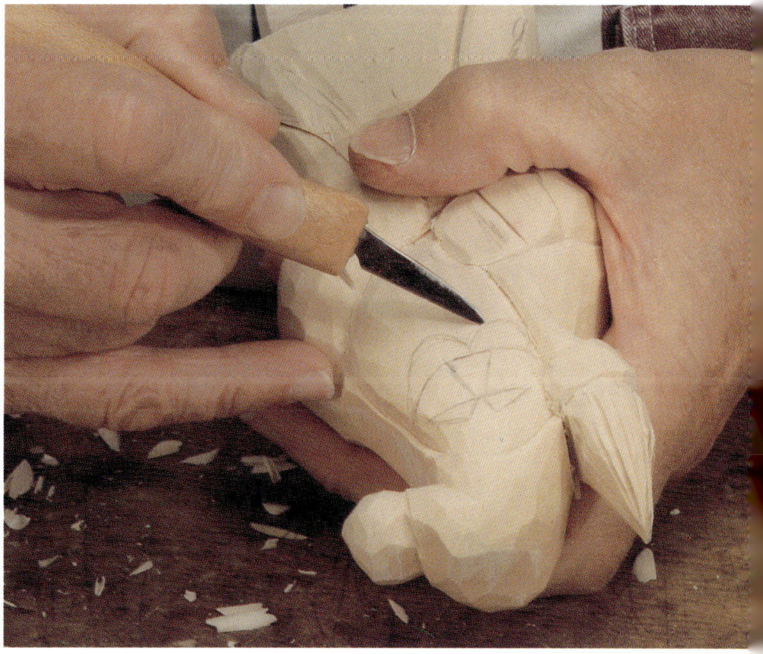

Incise under the mustache line.

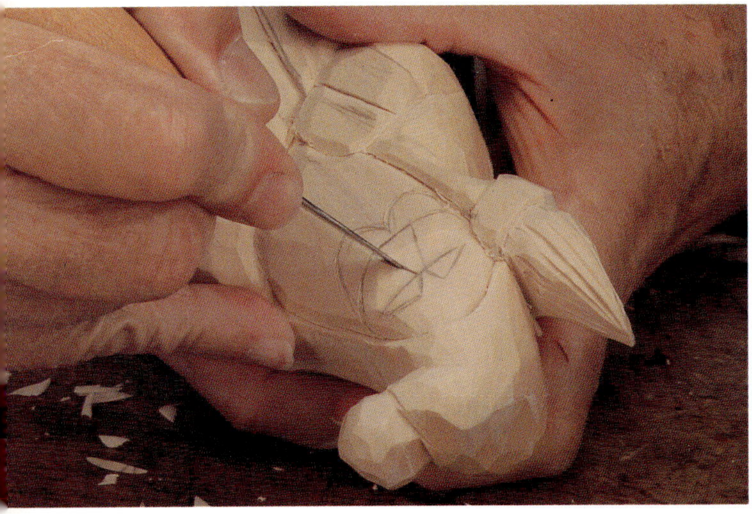

Make a nice cut down either side of the nose.

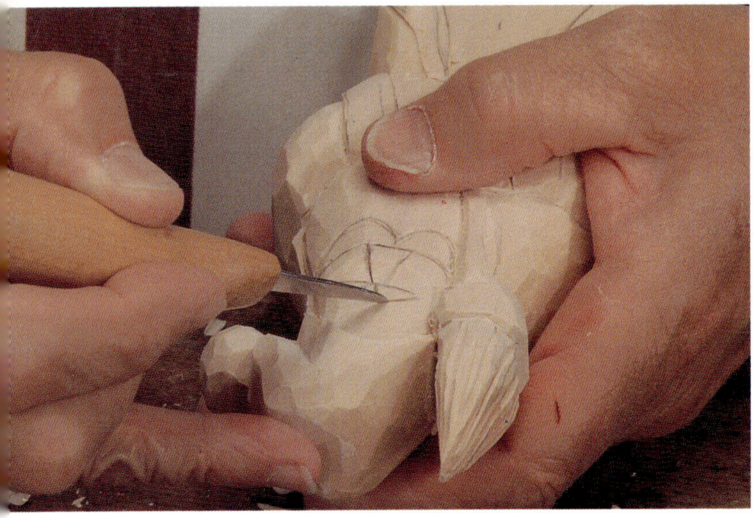

Be careful not to make too deep of a line on your eye-brows.

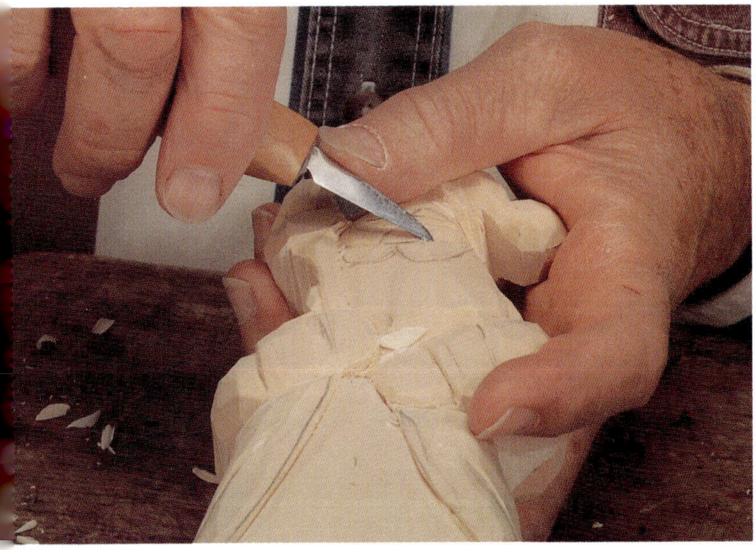

Round the little fat cheeks.

Remove each piece around the nose.

This is a larger face than the first Santa, so you have more to work with. Shape the nose.

Take out the pieces under each side of the mustache.

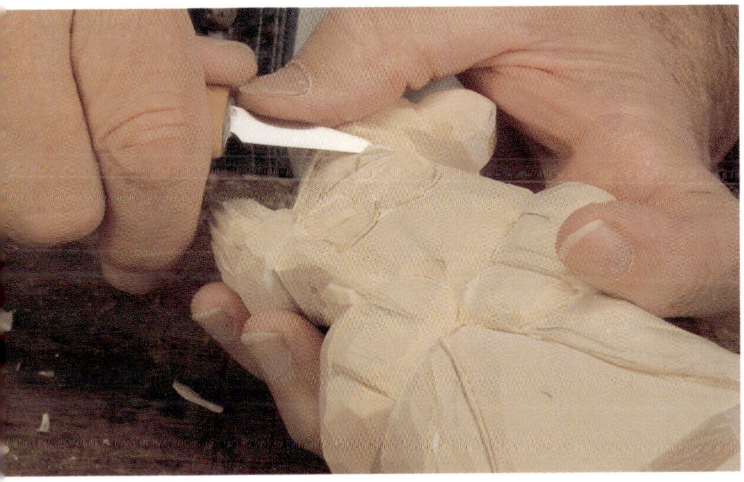

Carefully trim the eyebrow.

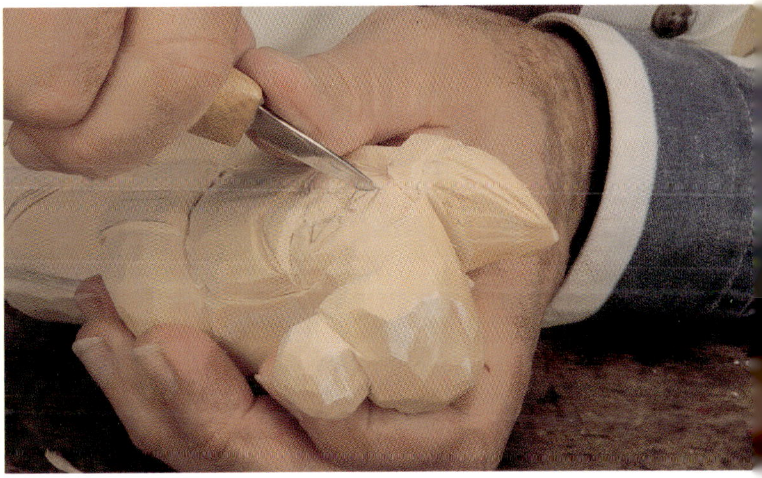

Stick knife deep into each corner of the eye.

Draw in the eyes.

Round the eye similar to what you did on the cheek, except on a smaller scale.

Note the difference in Santa's eyes on these two. On the left I have kept Santa's right eye shut to show he is squinting in the light of the torch. You can do this or keep both eyes open, as on the right.

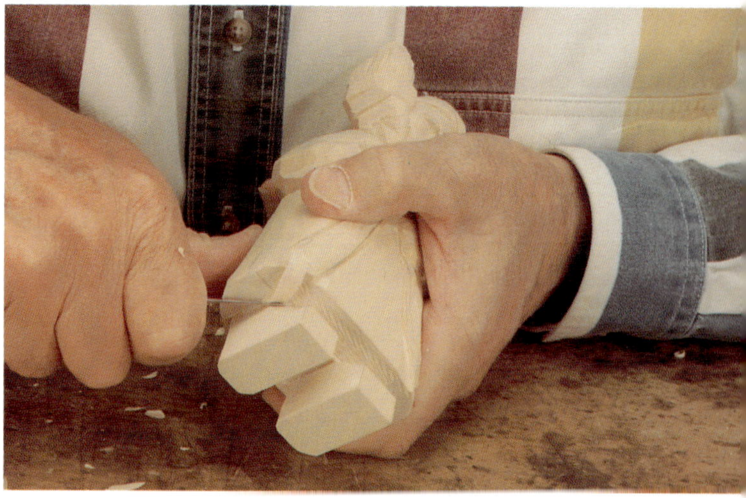

Whichever eye style you choose to do, make sure Santa's left eye remains open.

Round the top of each boot.

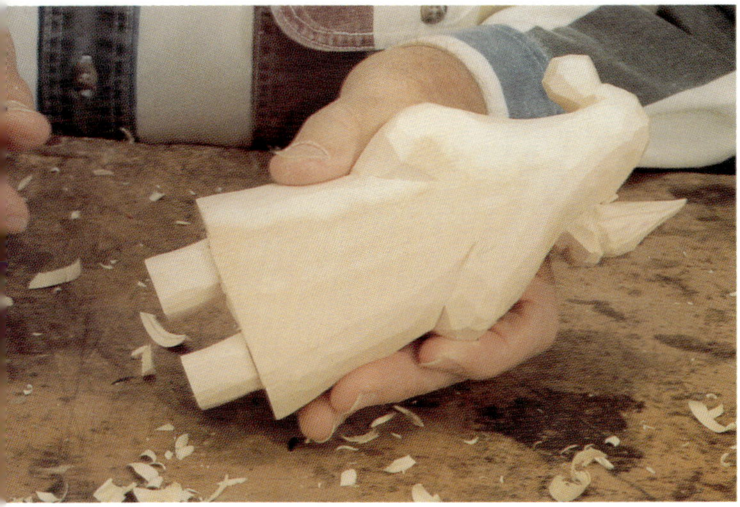

Round the backside.

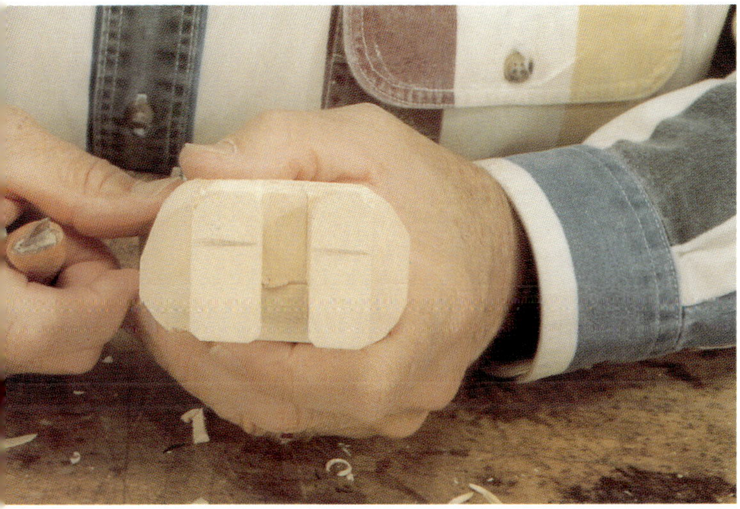

Draw in the heels.

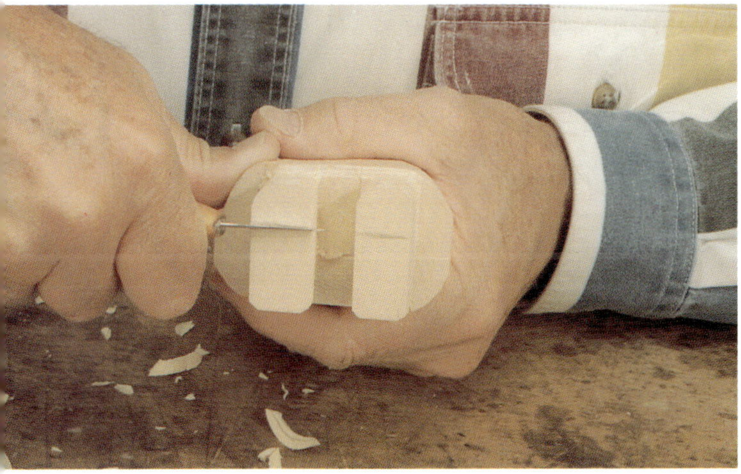

Rock the knife along the line you have drawn in.

Take a notch on each foot, inside of foot as well as outside.

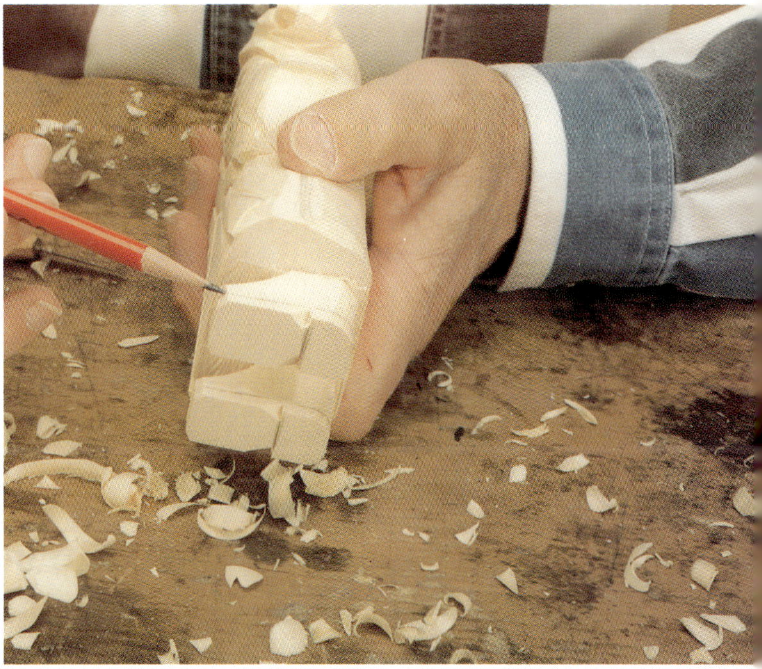

It may be helpful to draw in the lines for your soles.

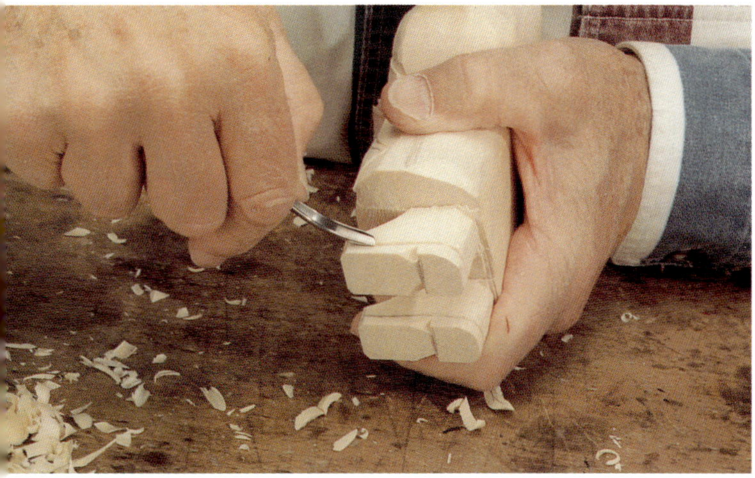

I am going to do one shoe with the small v-gouge and one using the knife. Here is the gouge.

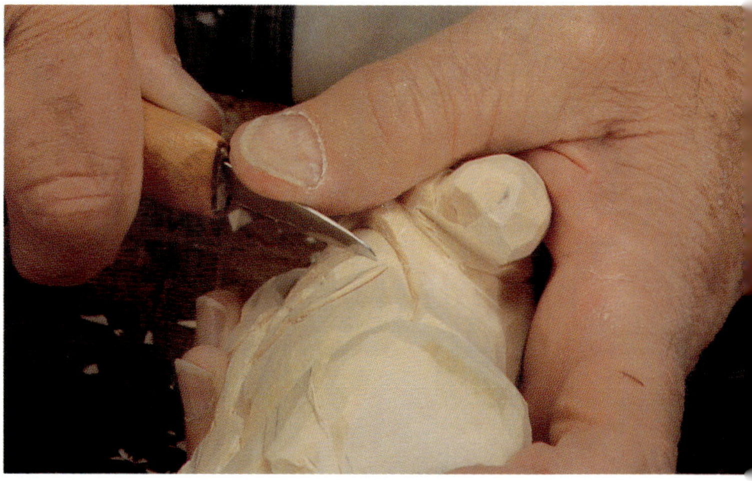

To put in the character lines just use the tip of your blade to make a small line.

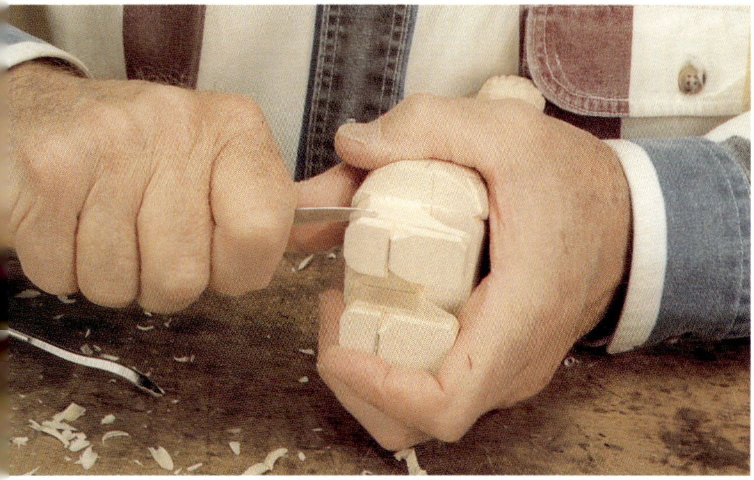

And with the knife, do another incise.

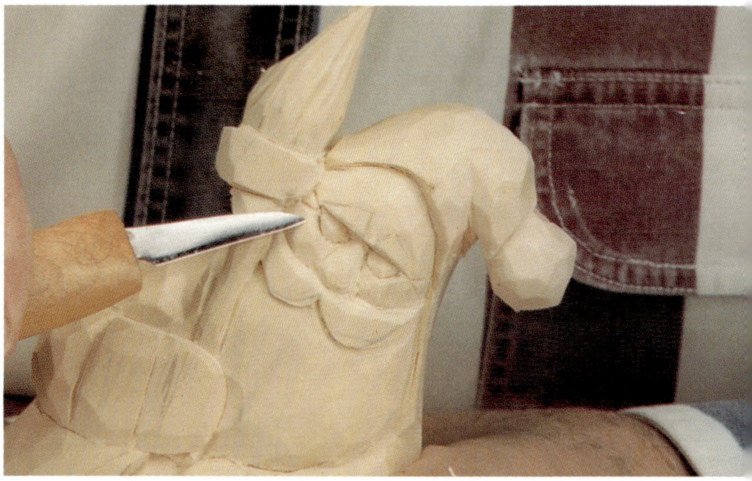

Do the same on the other side.

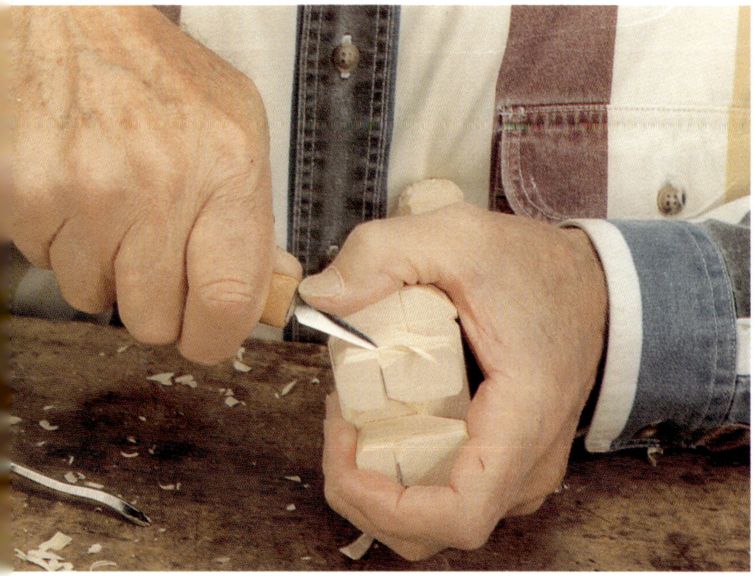

Come back next to the line and do another cut.

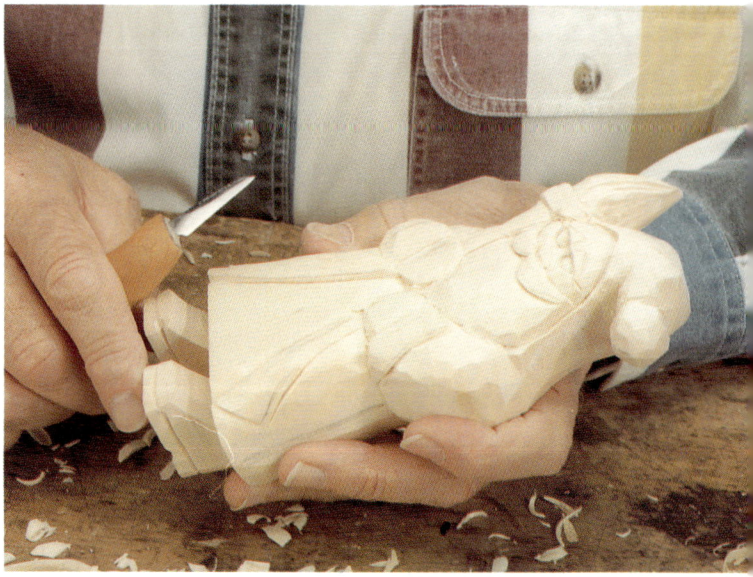

Go back and clean up in any rough areas you may have, until you feel you have finished piece ready to be painted.

Santa with Snowman

This pattern is reproduced at 85%.
To restore photocopy at 119%.

Our next Santa. Here he is in the process of building a snowman.

To help me along the way first I have drawn some guidelines.

Start by rounding his left shoulder.

Our third Santa, before and after.

Incise the line on the back of the arm.

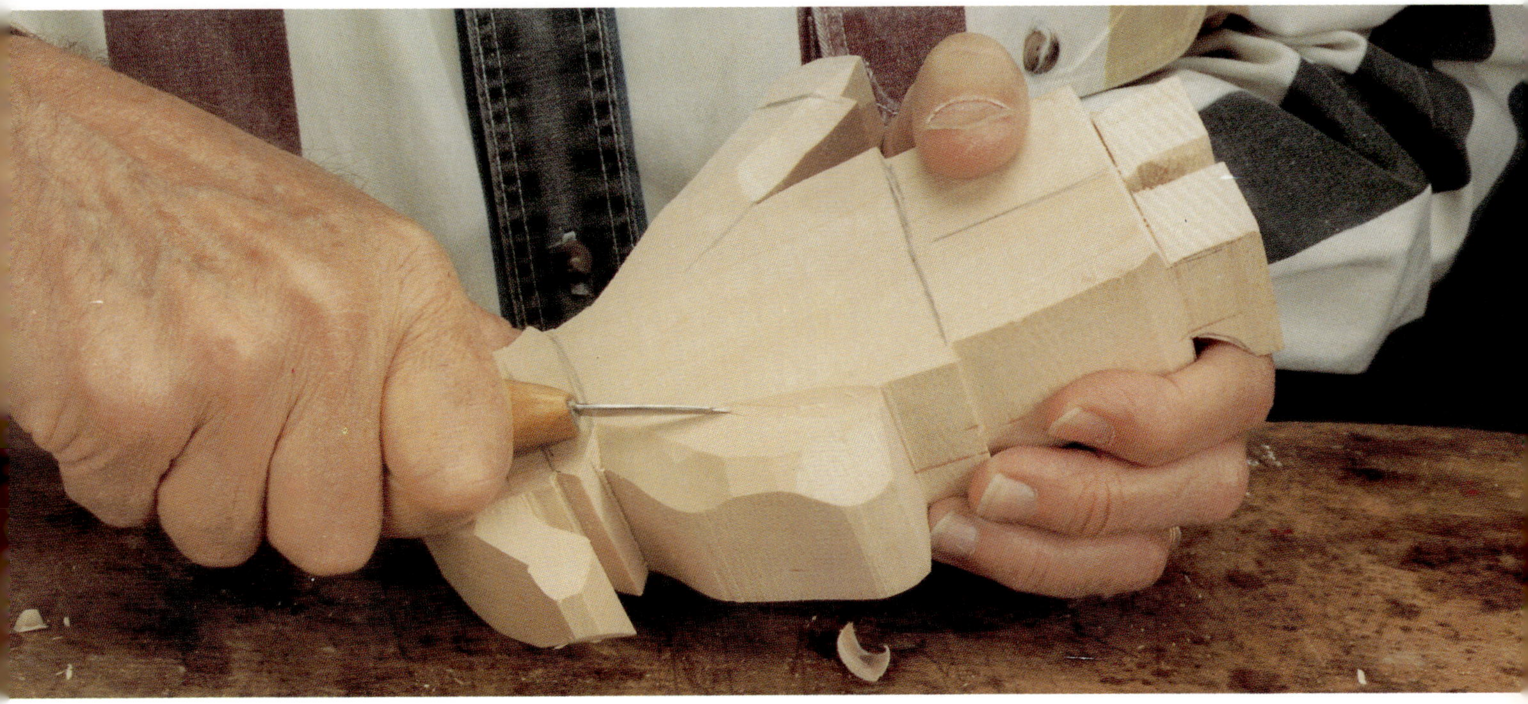

Take out that line with a large v-cut.

Round out his elbow.

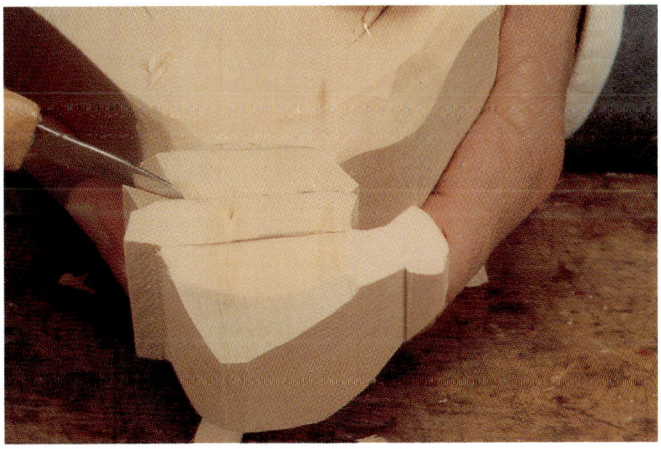

Trim up the back of the hairline.

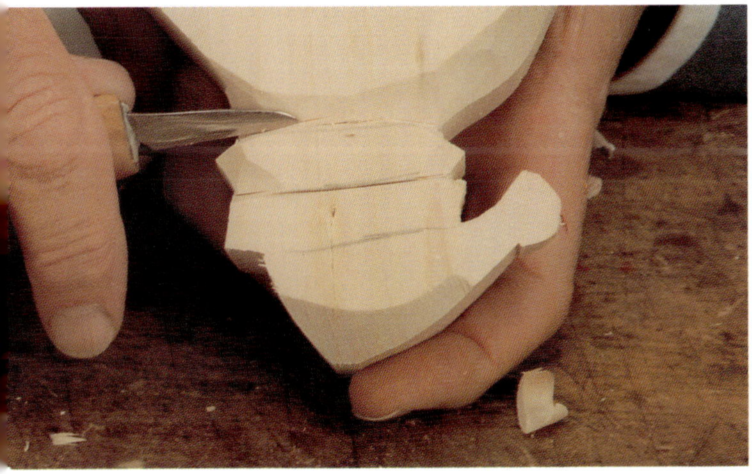

Incise the bottom of the hairline.

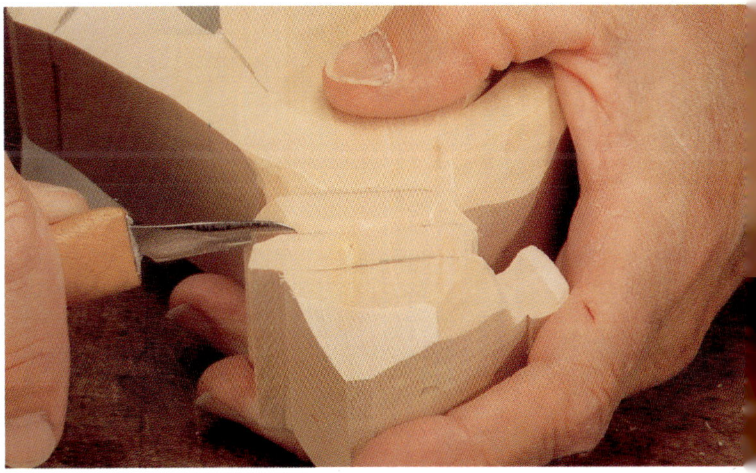

Incise the trim where hair goes into cap.

Round off the top of the cap.

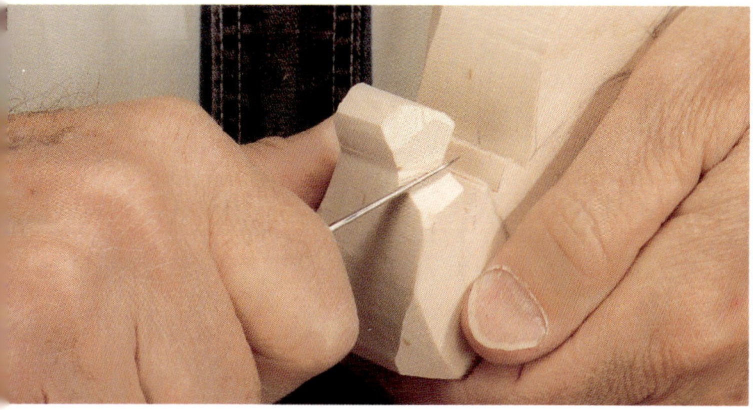

Make a series of v-cuts until you get the ball of the cap the size you want it.

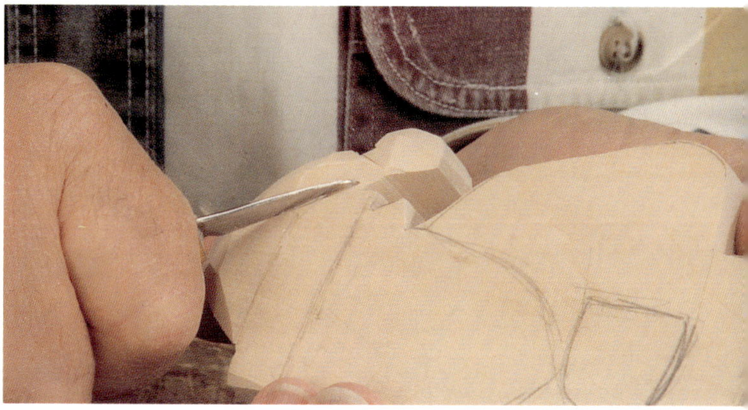

Make a v-cut where the cap flaps over.

Incise and continue to shape cap.

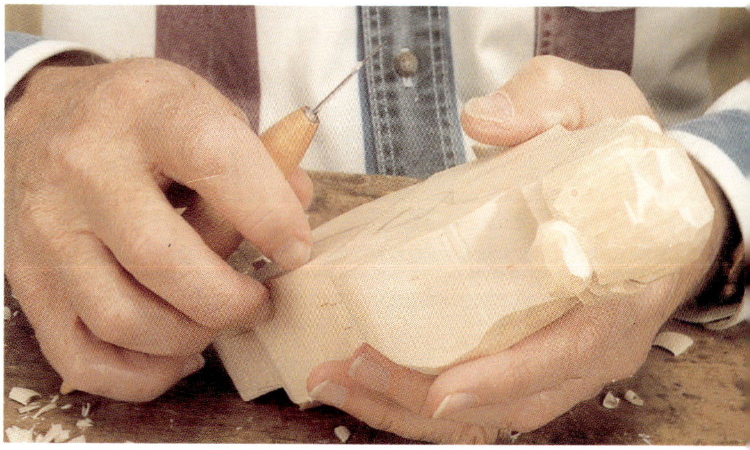

Continue to shape the cap.

Round the shoulder into the beard, leaving plenty of room for where your beard will go.

Do the left shoulder in the same manner.

You want the hairline to go back a ways, away from the beard.

Begin to round the shoulder. Continue to go over the entire piece and round out what you need to.

Incise the lines of Santa's trousers.

Take out the area between the legs and round out where the legs go into the boots.

The other side was done with a knife, so now here's how to do the same thing using a gouge. Continue rounding and shaping Santa.

Drill a hole for the scarf of the snowman.

We will put mittens instead of fingers on this Santa, as he is building a snowman and wants to keep his hands warm.

I have incised a line all the way around the bottom of his sweater.

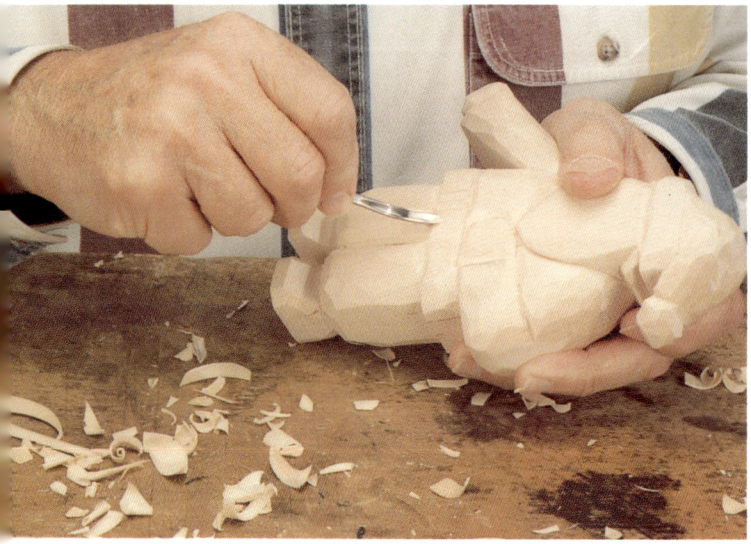

Put ribs along the bottom of the sweater and in the cap with your gouge. This can be done with a knife instead, but it is much easier to do it with a gouge. Also add ribs on the sleeves.

The finished ribs on the fringes of Santa's coat.

The completed face, done in the same way as the first two Santas shown in this book. Refer to the previous patterns if you need help.

Santa's snowman, before and after.

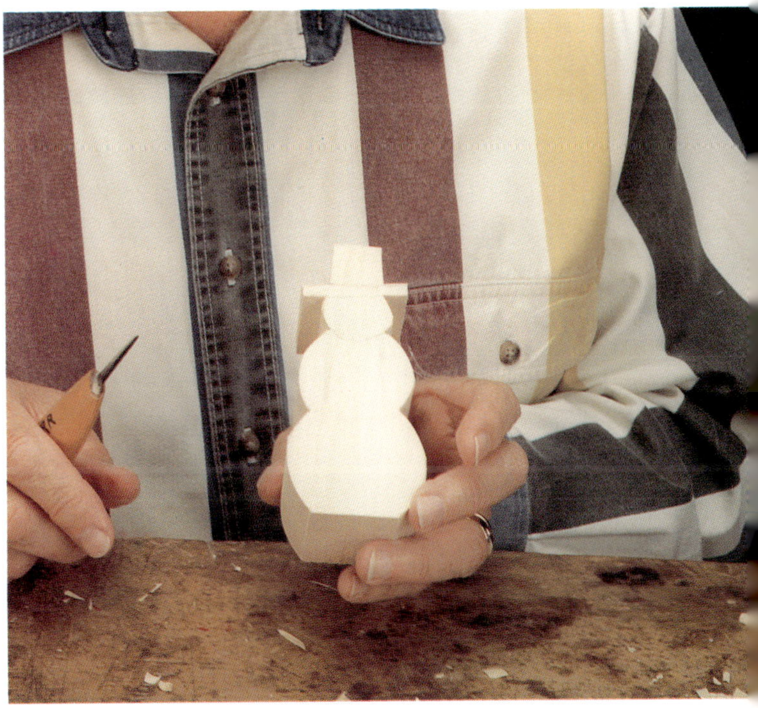

In the past few years, carving snowmen has become very popular, so here I will give you a few hints on how to make one.

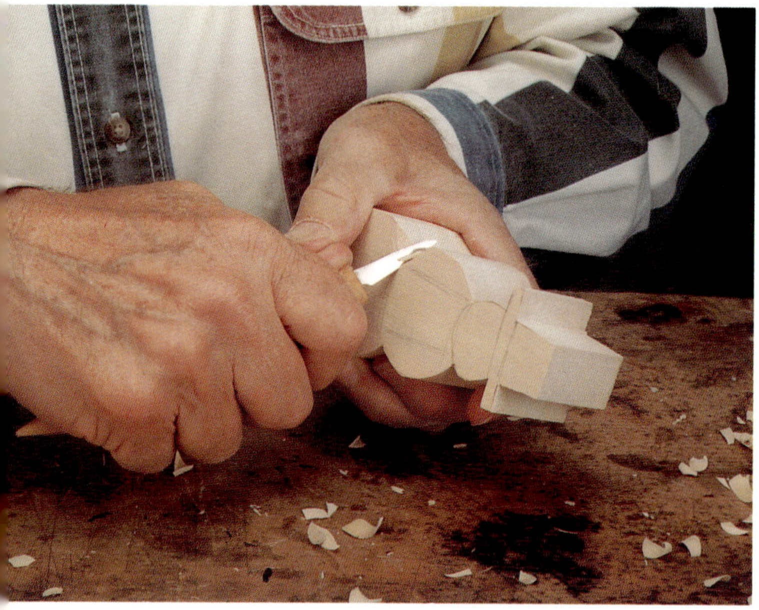

Cut around where the larger snowball is joined with the middle snowball.

Incise a line where the head goes into the hat.

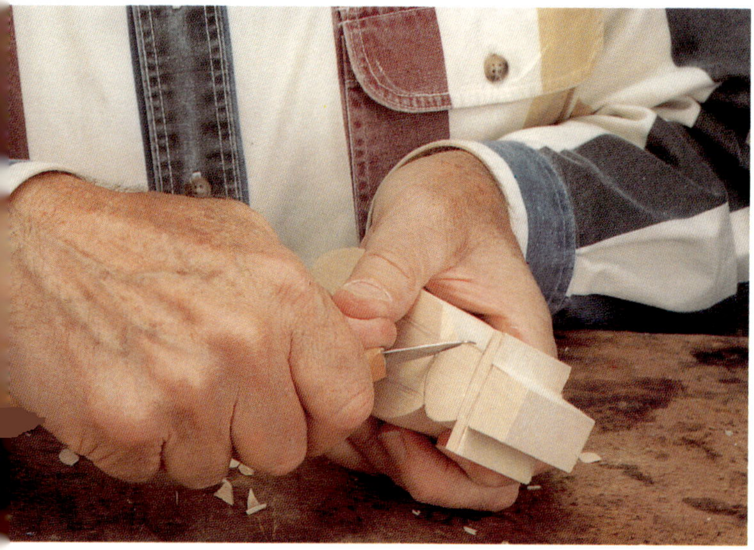

Do the same thing where the middle snowball meets the top snowball, then round the areas together.

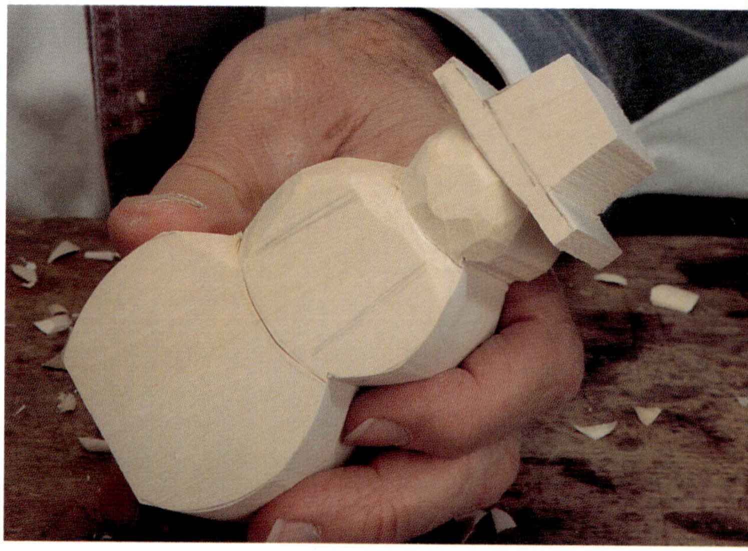

Round the head.

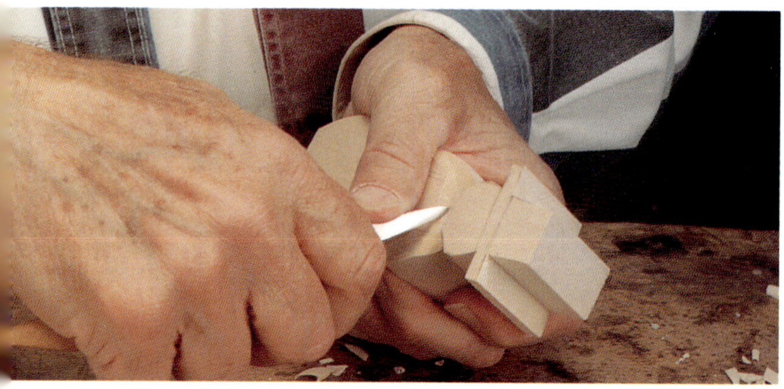

Cut under the chin of the snowman and round up.

Incise a line where the middle and bottom parts meet, and round them together.

This snowman is wearing a black vest to match his top hat, so we cut an area for the vest.

Make a couple of buttons with an eye punch.

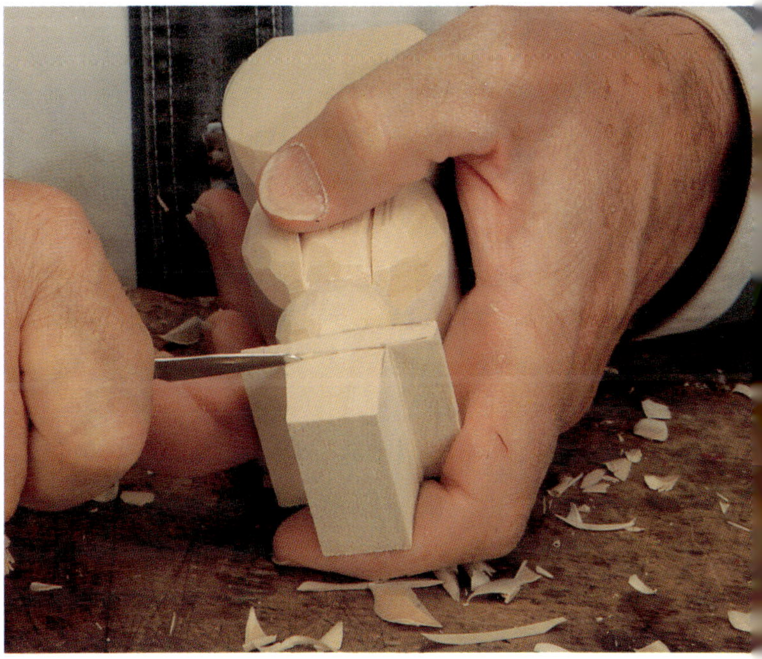

Incise a line for the top hat.

Round the crown of the hat and brim.

Use a punch to make the eyes and a small dowel for the carrot nose. You will notice that I did not give the snowman a mouth, because we will cover up that area with his scarf. I used little pieces of dogwood for the arms. I think you will have fun with the other snowman patterns shown in the pattern section.

Santa on Skis

Before and after Santas with skis.

On this Santa I will only hit the high points, as you should be ready for this one after doing the other three patterns in this book. You should know by now what I mean by incising and rounding.

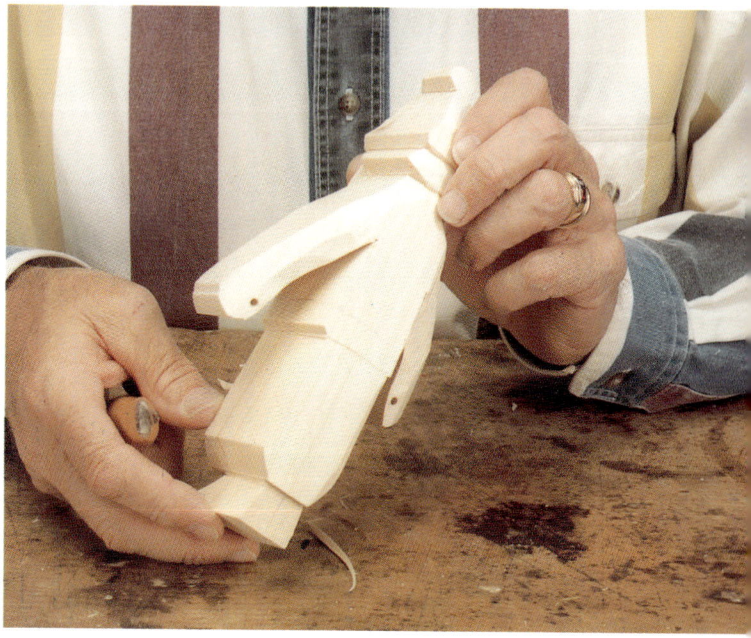

The arms on this Santa are at an angle, so it will take a little longer to trim them down to the size that you want.

I have separated the sleeve from the hand. Continue to trim down the arms.

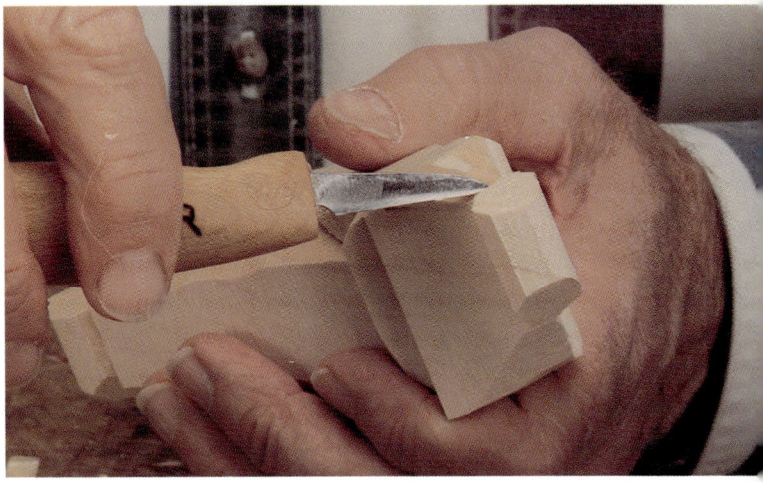

I have made the ball look like a ball.

An important part of this Santa is to make the beard prominent on either side

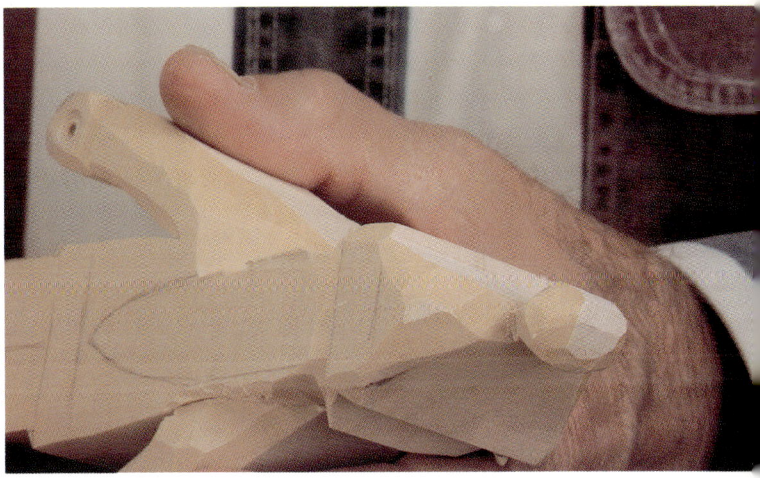

Continue rounding out the ball.

The ball of this hat is different from the others because it is on the top, so we will spend a little more time on it.

Incise the beard.

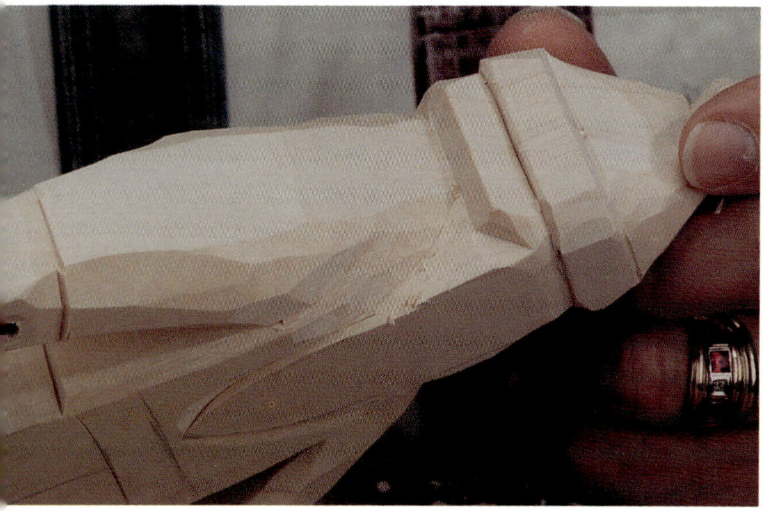

I have cut away from the beard.

Make a cut with the Flexcut tool to define his butt. Santa's knees are bent so his behind sticks out a little.

I'm now rounding and separating the legs.

Just make a small part on the two feet, back and front.

I'm using the Flexcut gouge to cut away behind the arm. The Flexcut gouge comes from the supplier sharpened and with minimum care on your buffing wheel they will remain sharp, and they are very flexible.

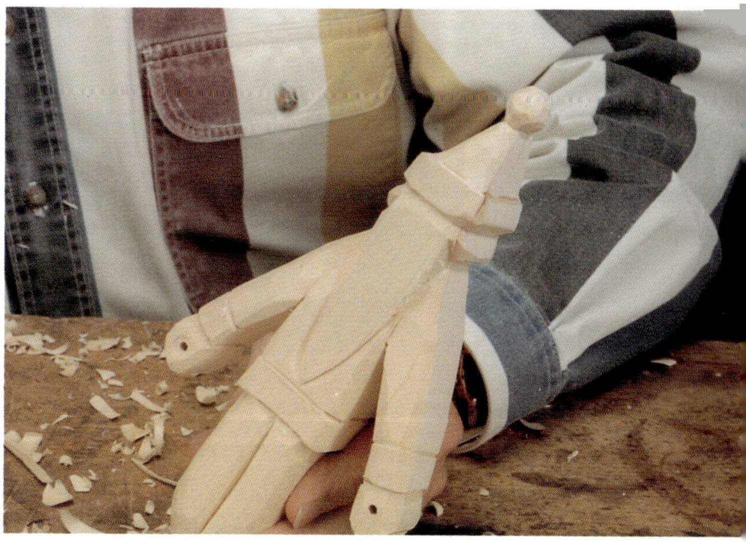

I have put the trim on the sweater and on the cap.

Put some wrinkles on the back side of his legs to show the bent knees.

Put a notch between the holes I have drilled for the ski poles and his hand.

I'm using the Flexcut gouge to do the soles of the ski boots.

I have put the line down the middle so I can round and get the egg shape of the face.

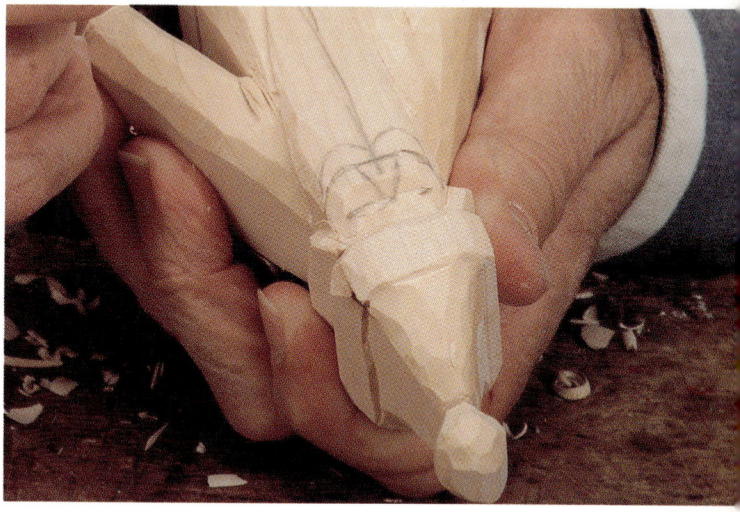

Draw the wide nose back in.

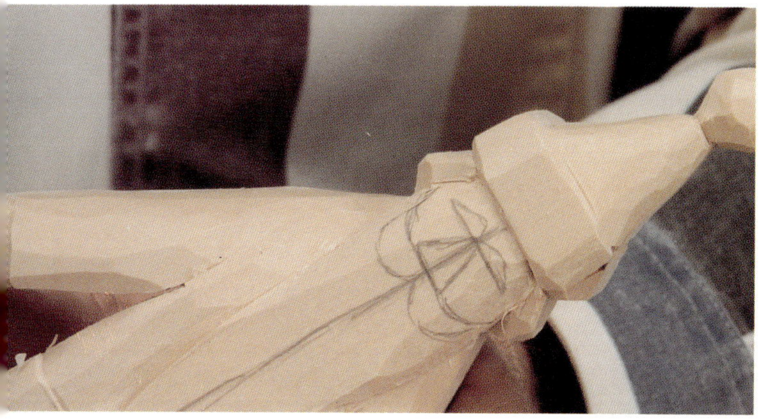

Having drawn in our lines, we are ready to start carving the face.

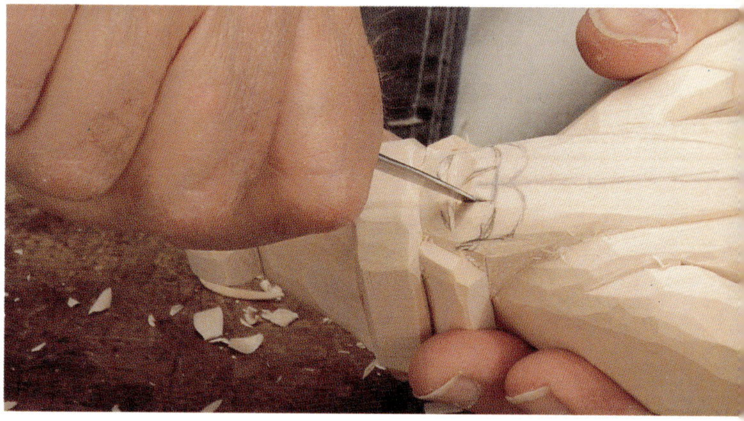

Do a nice deep cut on each side of the nose.

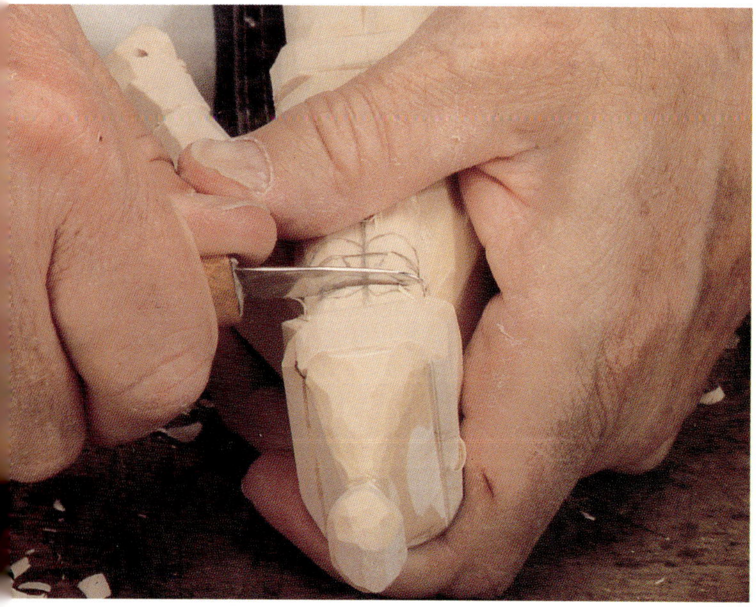

Take your knife across the horizontal line and round up to it.

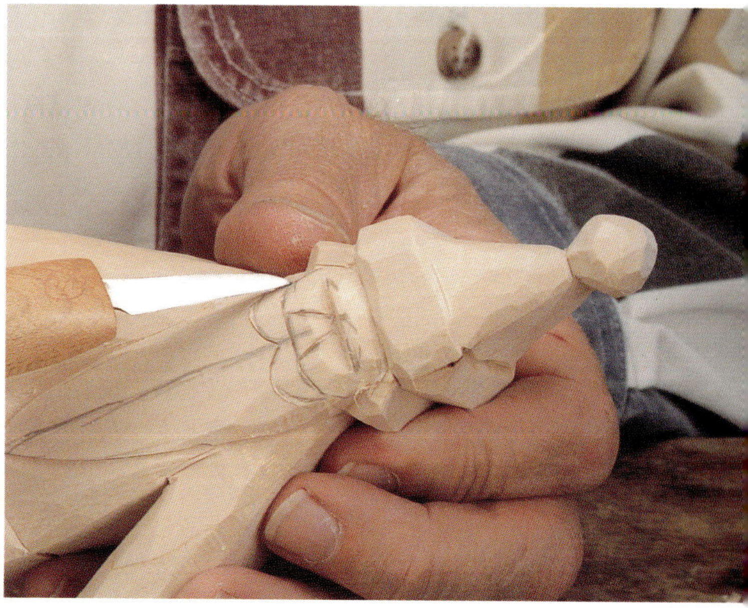

Incise around the cheek and moustache line.

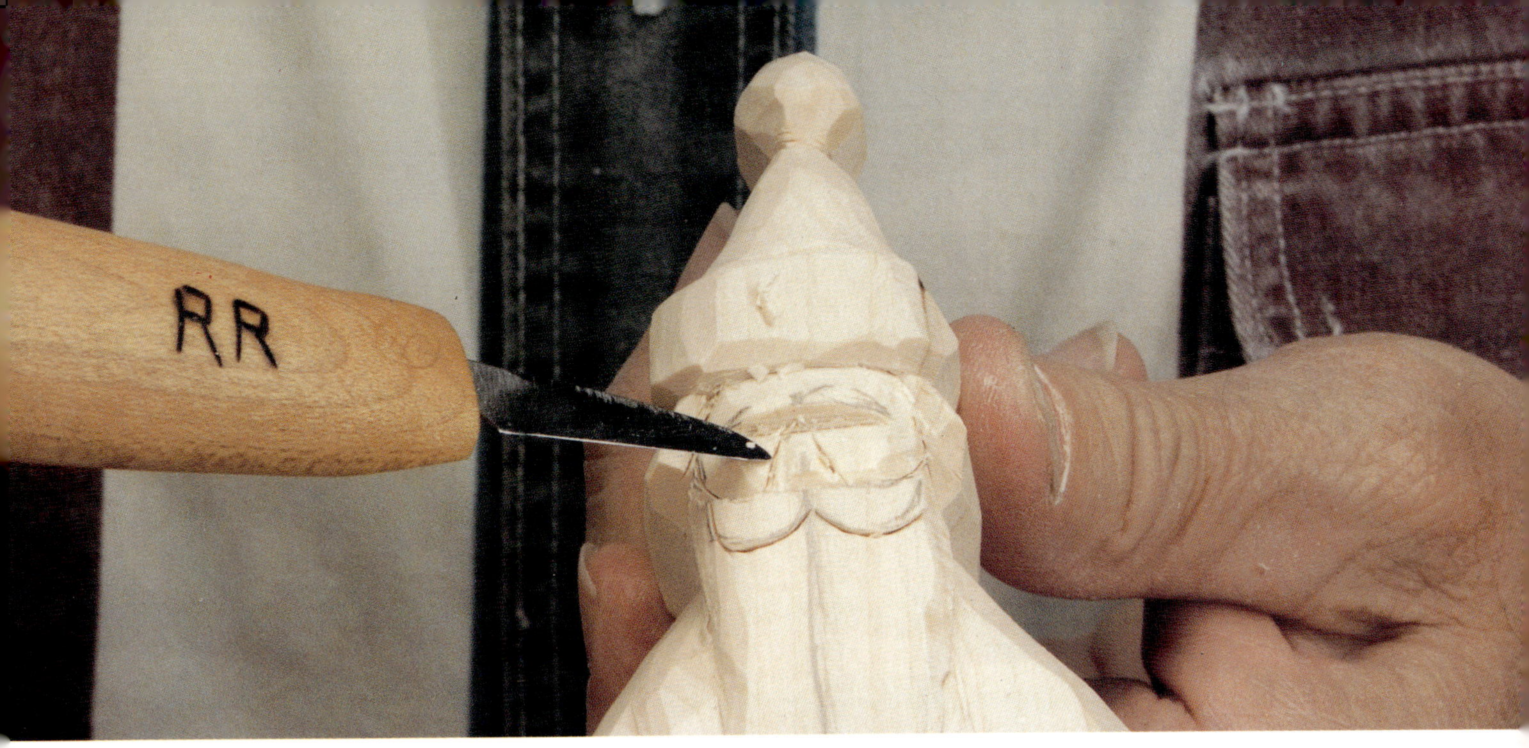

Cut around the nose.

Round the cheeks into the moustache.

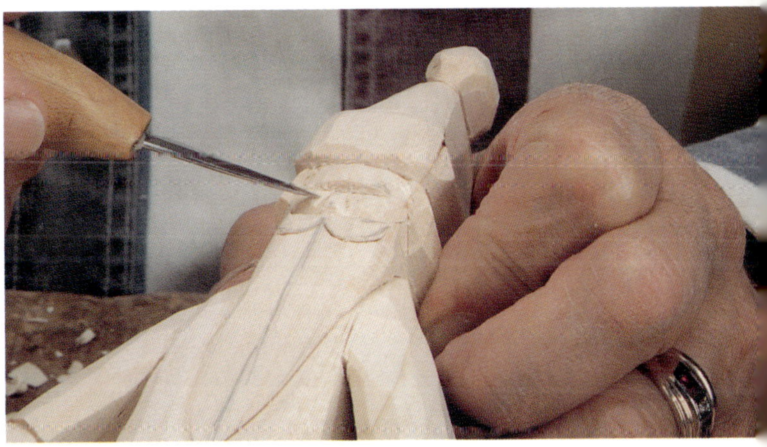

This is a good example of why we make a wide nose—a piece just chipped out of it and I had to go back and fix it.

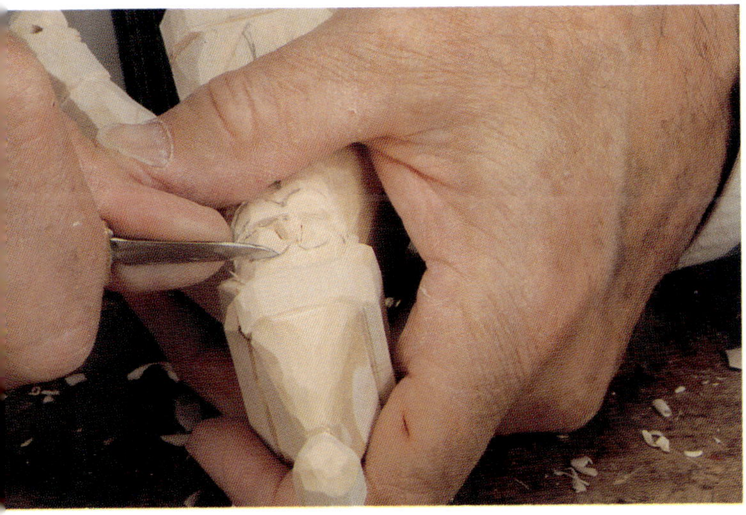

Incise into the eyebrows. I will paint in the eyes on this Santa because they are so small.

The ski poles are dowels with small wheels that I bought at the craft shop.

The skis are about 1/8" of an inch thick, and we draw a line down the middle and make a pair of skis out of this one piece of wood.

We put a little gouge cut down the middle.

Smooth out some of the rough edges and he will be ready to paint.

Just to whet your creative appetite: here is an example of one of my smaller Santas, shown to size. One of the landmarks in my home of Marietta, Georgia, is the "Big Chicken". Several years ago, the big hurricane came through and almost destroyed the chicken. When the restaurant chain that owned the business threatened to remove our chicken, the natives became restless and the landmark was built back better than ever. I do a cast necklace each year and, thank goodness, they have become collectible.

Painting

Here are the paints we will be using. They are acryllic paints, I prefer to use the Ceramcoat by Delta brand.

I am starting with Tompte red, painting the largest area first. Don't be concerned about your paint blending into the other areas, because once dry it can easily be fixed.

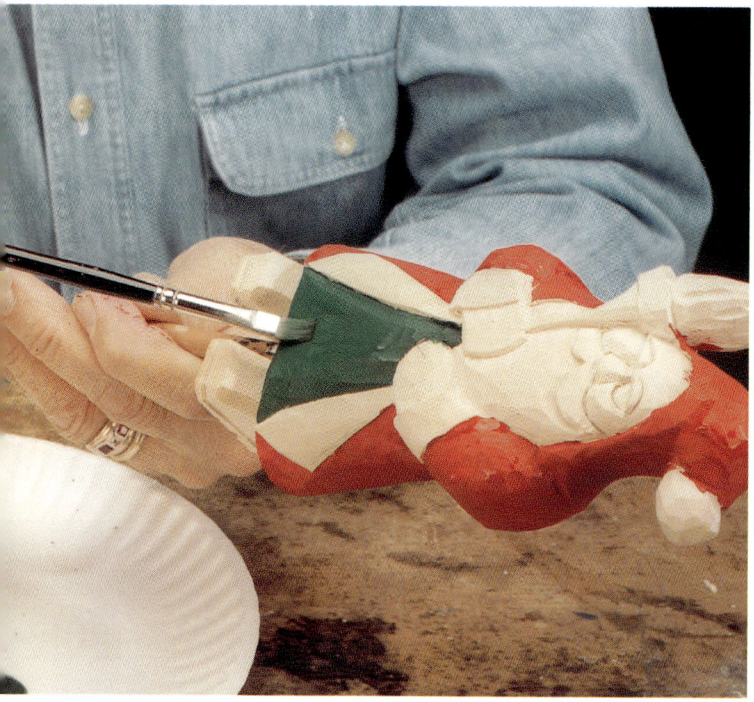

We will use the Santa with Torch to demonstrate painting techniques which can be used on all the Santas shown in this book. Use Hunter Green for the inner part of the robe.

I use Santa's Flesh paint for the face and other skin areas. It is almost the same color as the basswood, so be sure that you cover it all.

To get the blush for the cheeks, mix a little Santa's Flesh with your red.

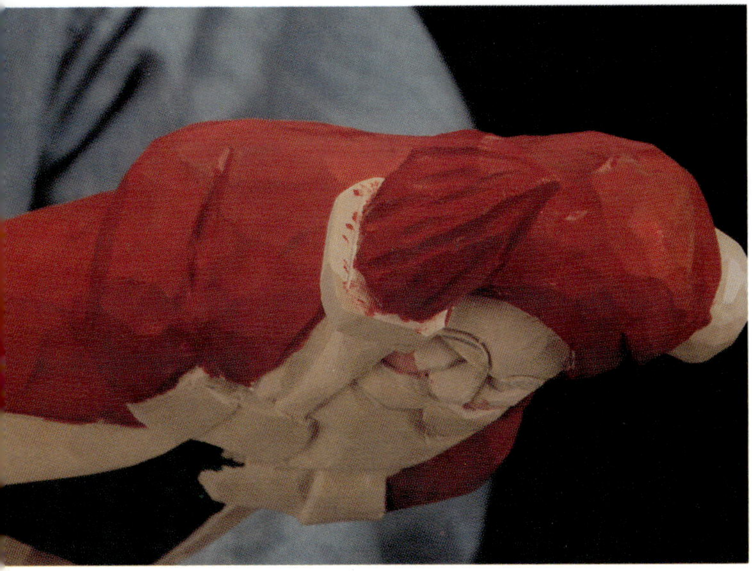

For painting the torch, first coat it with the red paint.

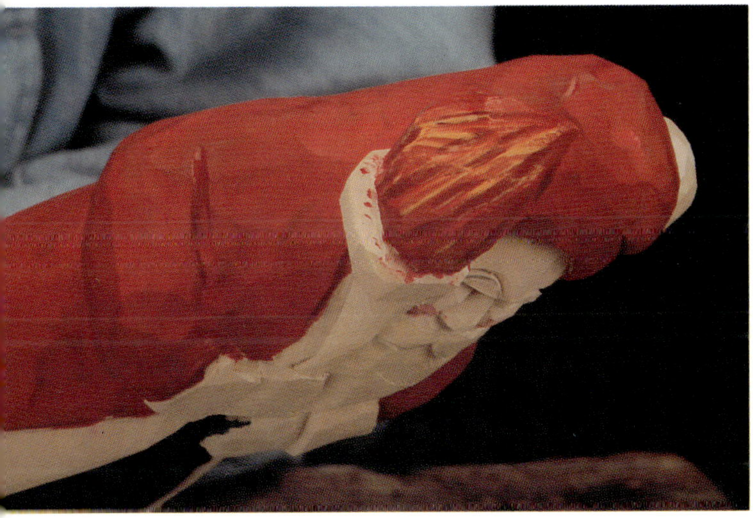

While it is still wet, highlight with the yellow paint.

Use Kim Gold for the torch.

Paint white on the beard and flap of robe, and black paint for the shoes.

The Santa with snowman is painted in the same manner, the snowman is white, and his cap can be any color you wish. Wrap a small piece of fabric around the snowman and through the hole in Santa's arm to make this duo complete. You'll notice that this is a different snowman from the one I illustrated being carved. You can paint all of the Santas in this book using the same techniques and paints.

Antiquing

Those of you who are familiar with my other methods of antiquing know that Griffin shoe polish is no longer available. If you are using Briwax and like the results, continue to use it. The method I am going to tell you about here is the method used by my friend Claude Bolton, cowboy carver extraordinaire.

Mix boiled linseed oil and turpentine or turpenoid half and half. Add a dab of burnt umber oil paint and shake. If you prefer a darker finish add more umber.

After your carving is painted and dry, paint on the mixture. After this dries, put a coat of Flecto brand Varathane diamond finish clear satin. The Varathane will protect as well as give a nice finish to your work.

I put my mixture in a covered (empty of course) mayo jar. Shake it before each use and it will last for a long time. I still prefer Ceramcoat acrylic paint from Delta Technical Coatings, Inc. I am a paint junkie and am fascinated by all the colors available. I have paint I've had for ten years and it still works fine.

The Gallery

RANSOM '97

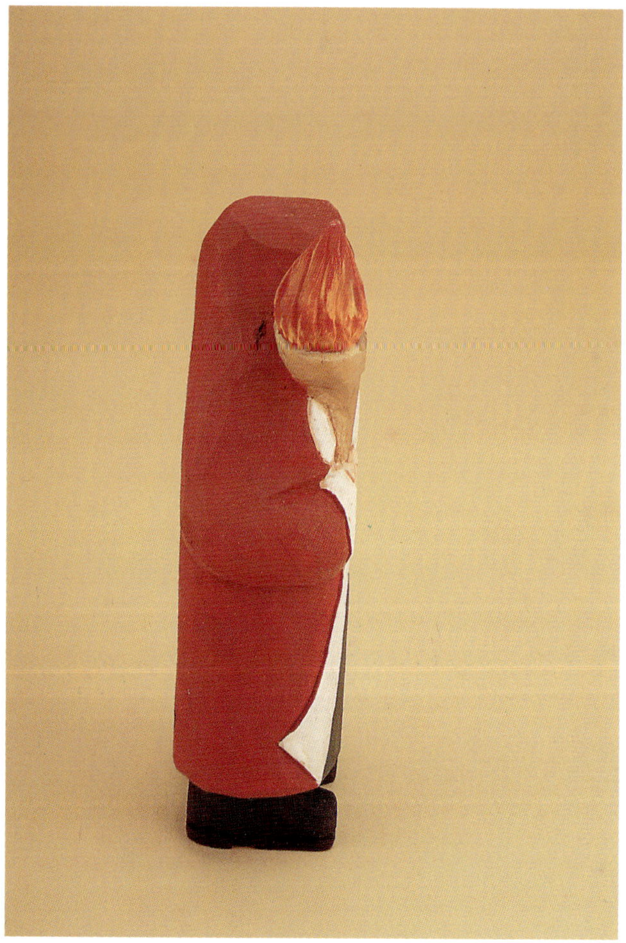

RANSOM '97
RANSOM '97

RANSOM
'97